WILL YOU MARRY ME?

*Discover
What it Means
to be
The Bride of Christ*

Laynie Travis

WESTBOW
PRESS®
A DIVISION OF THOMAS NELSON
& ZONDERVAN

WestBow Press books may be ordered through booksellers or by contacting:

WestBow Press
A Division of Thomas Nelson & Zondervan
1663 Liberty Drive
Bloomington, IN 47403
www.westbowpress.com
1 (866) 928-1240

ISBN: 978-1-9736-7017-9 (sc)
ISBN: 978-1-9736-7018-6 (e)

Library of Congress Control Number: 2019910715

Print information available on the last page.

WestBow Press rev. date: 11/06/2019

CONTENTS

Intro   Will You Marry Me? 1

Week 1   **Put a Ring on It** 7
     Day 1: Chosen 8
     Day 2: Purchased 12
     Day 3: Do You Take This Man? 15
     Day 4: Honeymoon Suite 19
     Day 5: I Now Pronounce You Husband and Wife 24

Week 2   **Ready or Not** 29
     Day 1: The Ten Virgins 30
     Day 2: Prepared 33
     Day 3: The Closed Door 36
     Day 4: Fear of Being Invited 38
     Day 5: Wardrobe Malfunction 42

Week 3   **The Bride, the Groom, and the Well** 47
     Day 1: Want to Grab a Drink? 48
     Day 2: She Says Yes 50
     Day 3: Isaac and Rebekah Tie the Knot 53
     Day 4: Love at First Sight 56
     Day 5: The In-Laws 59

Week 4   **Never the Bridesmaid, Always the Bride** 63
     Day 1: Han Solo 64
     Day 2: Party Foul 68
     Day 3: Drop the Mic 72

Day 4: Washed Clean 74
Day 5: First Miracle. 76

Week 5 A Match Made in Heaven 79
Day 1: The Cup of Acceptance 80
Day 2: Living Water. 83
Day 3: It's Complicated 86
Day 4: The Hour Has Come! 88
Day 5: I Am He 90

Week 6 Going to the Chapel 95
Day 1: The Rapture. 96
Day 2: The Glorious Appearing 100
Day 3: Two Become One 102
Day 4: It Is Finished, My Bride! 105
Day 5: Newlyweds 107

Laynie Travis is in love with Jesus, her husband, children, and spreading the good news of the gospel! She was saved at a young age and loves sharing the truth of Jesus. In the midst of raising her large family, Laynie felt the Lord nudge her to put her faith into action and start a Bible study in her local community. Suddenly, a new passion was born inside of her, and that one first step of faith has inspired her to not only teach, but also write Bible devotionals. Laynie published her first book, *Do You See This Woman?*, and plans to continue writing Bible studies for women. Laynie also hosts a podcast, "Gospel on the Go", offering short, power-packed bible messages in under 10 minutes.

Let's stay in touch! Visit my website, www.laynietravis.com
for updates and please follow me on social media.
Instagram: @laynietravis
Facebook:@authorlaynietravis
Twitter: @laynietravis

Will You Marry Me?

Just go with me here for a second. I have to warn you. I'm a hopeless romantic!

Picture yourself as a bride. The church doors open, and your eyes behold a sight so magnificent that you can't put the image into words. All your senses are awakened to a beauty and heightened feeling you can't contain. You're lost in the sound of music and blinded by the potent color, floating on the intensity of excitement and bursting with love and joy.

You're beautiful, and you know it. You're unashamed. You're ravishing and glowing. Your hair is smooth and tame, streaming in locks down your back. (Okay, I'm getting a little carried away, but we girls love good hair. I've never had good hair, so let a girl dream.)

You hear the sound of drums start to play loudly, and something compels you to start running unabashedly down the aisle. You pick up speed, and tears begin streaming down your face. You're not contained. You can't get to the end fast enough because you see Him, Jesus. He's at the end of the aisle smiling—even laughing. You're here! The wedding is here! The hour has come!

He's waiting for you, and He's standing there with arms open wide. Let me add that He's beautiful. He's more than beautiful. He's cool and gorgeous. He might even have a man bun and tattoos. He's nothing like the Jesus you've seen in church photos. (Forgive me. Lately I've been into man buns. Just saying!)

You no longer care about the dress. Your shoes come off, you're now barefoot, and your hair flies everywhere as you leap into His arms. He has you! Yes, you! The girl who never thought she was beautiful, the girl who failed, the girl who was afraid she didn't make the cut, the girl who just knew His love wouldn't last, the girl who didn't think she had it in her, the girl who had given up on love. You!

He wants you, and He's waiting for you to say yes. You're His bride. You belong to Him. He died for you, and He has the scars to prove it. Even in your shame, your sin, and your failures, you're all He's ever wanted. Say yes! Your hour has come!

God uses metaphors all throughout the Bible to give us pictures of what our relationship with Him looks like. He's our heavenly Father, and He calls us His sons and daughters. He calls us His friends and lays down His life for us. He's our Savior that rescues His people from their sins. He's our king, and we're members of His kingdom. He's the Good Shepherd, and we are His sheep. He's the tabernacle, and we're the living stones. We're all members of one body, and He's the head. The Bible is full of relational imagery that give us pictures of what our relationship to Him should look like.

In this study, we're going to focus on a unique and special metaphor that God uses in over one hundred verses across the Old and New Testaments. He refers to Himself as our Bridegroom and us as His bride. He doesn't just want to rule over us as a king or know us just as a Father. He wants a love relationship with us. His love will exceed every form of relationship we experience here on earth. He's our friend, father, lover, teacher, healer, redeemer, and Savior. However, the love relationship that Jesus wants with us as individuals and as a church is special.

It's an intimate, reciprocating love. He's jealous for us. He wants us as a husband wants his bride. He adores us and desires to be in complete unity with us. He longs for His bride and fights for her to the point that He laid down His life to be with her. It doesn't matter if you're single or married. Our marriage to Jesus will exceed our expectations of any physical marriage we have here on earth. He uses the model of marriage to give us a picture of perfect intimacy and reciprocating love in the spiritual realm. 1 Corinthians 2:9 (NLT) tells us, "No eye has seen, no ear has heard, and no mind has imagined what God has prepared for those who love him."

God designed marriage. At the beginning of the Bible, we see that in the garden of Eden, a man named Adam was formed and a woman named Eve was formed out of his rib. In Genesis 2:24 (NIV), we read, "A man leaves his father and mother and is united to his wife, and they become one flesh."

This was God's design from the beginning. They were unified, naked, and unashamed. They were two halves that came together to become whole. They were completely and utterly exposed, both physically and emotionally, and both felt safe. They had nothing to hide. Adam and Eve enjoyed perfect fellowship with one another and with God.

God is whole and complete; however, He wants to unify with us. He doesn't need us. He wants us. The garden was unpolluted by sin until the evil serpent, Satan, deceived Adam and Eve and sin entered the world. The perfect fellowship between God and man and between husband and wife was then broken and needed to be fixed to restore fellowship. Adam and Eve felt shame, realized they were naked, and hid from God.

Jesus came to earth to save us, take away our sin and shame, and restore what was broken. We're His people (His bride), and He's our Bridegroom, coming to purify us and get us ready for the great wedding and feast that awaits us in eternity. He wants us! He's down on one knee begging for us and fighting for us to say yes!

In this study, we're going to grasp a greater understanding of the love relationship we have in Christ. We'll soon discover that there's a coming wedding and celebratory feast like none we could ever dream of. We're going to look week by week into the wedding language used in the Bible and see how it applies it to us spiritually today.

In the first week, we'll look at a physical picture of marriage mirrored in the spiritual realm. We'll begin laying a foundation of the bride-groom relationship by studying the Jewish wedding culture and process. I promise it won't be boring. In the second week, we'll study two parables (biblical stories with a moral lesson) that better explain the coming wedding and what our role is now. In the third week, we'll look at how two patriarchs (founding fathers) of our faith give us a visual picture of the Jewish wedding custom and see the many parallels of our love relationship with Christ.

In the fourth week, we'll study the significance of Jesus performing His first miracle at a wedding turning water into wine (cheers!) and what that symbolizes. In the fifth week, we'll see who the bride of Christ is (spoiler alert: it's us) and how we become betrothed to marry Him. Don't worry! I'll explain all the fancy words along the way. Finally in the sixth week, we'll learn about the coming wedding and all we as believers have to look forward to in the feast and celebration.

Let's go, girls!

About the Study

Join me in the six-week study, and let's discover what it means to be the Bride of Christ.

- The first video session is an introduction to the series.

- Each week we'll look at stories and parables from the Bible that symbolize what our love relationship with Christ looks like both here on earth and for all eternity.

- In the second and following weeks, we'll gather as a group and view a teaching video followed by group discussion.

- This study is designed to bring women together. I encourage you to find a group or step out in faith and form a group!

- All teaching videos can be found at www.laynietravis.com/willyoumarryme

- If you need help or encouragement along the way, please reach out to me at hello@laynietravis.com.

Group Guide

- Welcome the Group

- Open in Prayer

- Watch Introduction video found at LaynieTravis.com/willyoumarryme (23:31)

- Go over discussion questions or as many as time allows for:

  1. Why do you think the world is so intrigued with weddings?
  2. What are some of your favorite wedding movies?
  3. Why do you think Jesus would use a wedding analogy in over 100 Bible verses to describe the relationship between God and mankind?
  4. What is a bridegroom?
  5. Who is the bride of Christ?
  6. Have you felt the pursuit of Jesus in your own life? If so, can you share a personal example?
  7. Read 2 Corinthians 11:2 aloud. What do you think this verse means?
  8. Have you ever studied this topic before?
  9. What is one key takeaway point from today's study?
  10. What are you most excited about learning through this study?

- Close in Prayer

WEEK 1

Put a Ring on It

Day 1: Chosen

It's important to understand the customs of a Jewish bride in the ancient Jewish culture to fully appreciate the symbolism between the bride and bridegroom of that time and how we fit into this picture. So let's pretend that we're going back in time. And just for fun, I'm going to invent a fictional couple to walk us through the Jewish wedding process.

Let's call the young unmarried couple Jack and Diane. (Okay. We've all heard the song! "A little ditty about Jack and Diane …" I had to throw that in there.) Let's say that Jack is a young Jewish farmer twenty years of age and Diane is an eighteen-year-old Jewish maiden. Ah, to be eighteen again.

Diane would be expected to be married to a Jewish man and not to a man of another religion or culture. Jack would probably already be aware that Diane was a prospect, and it quite possibly would have been discussed by both sets of parents when they were very young; however, now that they're of age, they're involved in the process.

Let's say that Jack and Diane run into one another at the village well. Wells were usually located outside a village and were known as meeting places or social hubs. Women took frequent trips to the well to gather water for their families, and men came to grab a drink or rest from a long day's work. The wells were the community social spots where young women and men could linger, visit, and not be under the watchful eye of their parents. They were kind of like a modern-day Starbucks!

Back to the story. Let's say that Jack, the farmer, learns when Diane, the maiden, would be coming to gather water and happens to be there grabbing a drink. Their eyes meet, and there's definitely some chemistry going on between them. They make small talk, and it's all he needs to know that she's the woman he wants as his bride.

In this culture, the wedding process was divided into two parts: the betrothal, comparable to our modern-day engagement, and the marriage ceremony and feast. We're going to unpack this intricate process using our fictional characters and discover how this ancient wedding custom gives us a mental picture of what our spiritual relationship with Christ looks like. It truly is fascinating. Let's dive in!

For starters, Jack would hold almost all the responsibility of planning and paying for the wedding. Do I need to say that again? Yes, you heard me right. The man was the wedding planner. Ladies, I think we may want to rethink how we do weddings here in our culture. *Can I get an amen?*

The first step in the Jewish wedding process was the betrothal, which is similar to our engagement period, but it has some crucial differences. This would begin with the groom's father choosing a suitable bride for him. Now Jack could and most likely would have a say (ahem, Diane), but the father did the final choosing.

Next, the father and his son would approach the chosen girl's family and present a marriage contract called a *ketubah,* meaning "contract" in Hebrew. The presentation of the *ketubah* was his way of asking permission from Diane and her family to begin what is known as the betrothal process. The contract would include promises that Jack would keep for her, and it would lay out the provisions he would make for her.

This betrothal process is different from an engagement in our modern-day culture because it was a binding contract. The couple would be legally married when this contract was signed. (Talk about signing your life away!) This would mean that the couple belonged to one another by law; however, they would not consummate the marriage until after the wedding ceremony, the second stage of the process. We'll get to that in the next couple of days. Ending the betrothal would require a divorce or—worse—death. It wasn't something the bride or groom could just casually change their minds about. This was a huge decision.

Read Matthew 1:18–20 and answer these questions:

- Were Mary and Joseph married? (We're now talking about real people!)

- What was Joseph going to do before he understood that Mary was pregnant supernaturally?

Exactly! They were betrothed (married by contract only). They were promised to one another, and these contracts were rarely broken. Both parties would willingly enter this contract and wait for a period until the day their marriage ceremony arrived. During this betrothal period, the man and woman could not be seen together, and wedding preparations would be in the works. So going back to our fictional couple, if Diane said yes, she wouldn't see Jack until he came to get her for the ceremony.

Take a minute to read the verses below and jot down the parallels you find between these first steps in the betrothal process and our faith walk. These verses pertain to us and Jesus.

> For he chose us in him before the creation of the world to be holy and blameless in his sight. (Ephesians 1:4 NIV)

> You did not choose Me but I chose you, and appointed you that you would go and bear fruit, and that your fruit would remain, so that whatever you ask of the Father in My name He may give to you. (John 15:16 NASB)

> For many are called, but few are chosen. (Matthew 22:14 ESV)

> So then you are no longer strangers and aliens, but you are fellow citizens with the saints, and are of God's household. (Ephesians 2:19 NASB)

Can you see it? God the Father chooses us for His Son, Jesus, just as the Jewish father chooses a bride for his son. God chooses all of us. If He made you, which He did, then He chose you, but it's a two-way street. Do we choose Him too?

Let's now look at a few verses that mention the betrothal.

> For I feel a divine jealousy for you, since I betrothed you to one husband, to present you as a pure virgin to Christ. (2 Corinthians 11:2 ESV)

> And I will betroth you to me forever. I will betroth you to me in righteousness and in justice, in steadfast love and mercy. I will betroth you to me in faithfulness. And you shall know the Lord. (Hosea 2:19–20 ESV)

> Therefore a man shall leave his father and mother and hold fast to his wife, and the two shall become one flesh. (Ephesians 5:31 ESV)

Now the birth of Jesus Christ took place in this way. When his mother Mary had been betrothed to Joseph, before they came together she was found to be with child from the Holy Spirit. (Matthew 1:18 ESV)

Do you see the resemblance? Hopefully these verses help familiarize us with this betrothal process. We're just getting started, but God set up the Jewish wedding picture to be an image of our relationship with Him. Jesus is the best teacher. He used a common custom of the day to give us a picture of what our love relationship with Him looks like.

Trust me. It gets better. Over the next few days, we're going to continue learning about the steps in this intricate process and then apply them to our spiritual walk. For now, know this. *You were chosen.*

> **Note:** To learn more about the Jewish betrothal and wedding process, check out the book *Chosen and Cherished: Becoming the Bride of Christ* by Edna Ellison, Joy Brown, and Kimberly Sowell. It's a great resource that helped inform this study.

Day 2: Purchased

Hi, girls! We're covering some great stuff today, so grab a cup of coffee or a Diet Coke—I drink both beverages regularly—and let's get going!

Remember our fictional characters Jack, the farmer, and Diane, the Jewish maiden? We left off yesterday talking about the first few steps in the Jewish wedding process. And today, we're picking up with the next step, called the bride price or *mohar*.

So far, Jack and his father have chosen Diane to be Jack's bride. They're now presenting her and her family with the *ketubah* (binding marriage contract) and talking numbers.

How much is she worth? Jack—the bridegroom or the groom-to-be—would pay a price for Diane. This sounds kind of weird, but it was a way to protect the woman in that day. The husband was obligated to provide for her and take care of her, so he would pay her family. If the bridegroom couldn't afford her, he would work for her to earn her for himself. Remember Jacob in the Bible? Let's take a look.

Read Genesis 29:14–30.

- How long did Jacob work for Rachel? (Remember that these are real people.)

Let's read some more verses and see what parallels can be drawn between this couple and us today.

> Christ bought us with His blood and made us free from the Law. In that way, the Law could not punish us. Christ did this by carrying the load and by being punished instead of us. (Galatians 3:13–15 NLV)

> You were bought with a price. Therefore honor God with your bodies. (1 Corinthians 6:20 NIV)

> For he has rescued us from the kingdom of darkness and transferred us into the kingdom of his dear Son, who purchased our freedom and forgave our sins. (Colossians 1:13–14 NLT)

> Keep watch over yourselves and all the flock of which the Holy Spirit has
> made you overseers. Be shepherds of the church of God, which he bought
> with his own blood. (Acts 20:28 NIV)

Just as Jack paid his bride price for Diane, Jesus paid a price for us. Jesus didn't purchase us
with money though. He purchased us with His blood. He died a brutal death for us to free
us from the dominion of darkness and rescue us from our sin.

Read Genesis 2:18–25.

- What happened after Adam and Eve sinned?

Adam and Eve were naked in the garden and felt no shame. They were naked physically
and emotionally, and they had perfect union with God. If you read on, you see that the
serpent, Satan, deceived Adam and Eve. At that moment, sin entered the world and severed
humanity's perfect relationship with God.

As a result, Adam and Eve realized that they were naked physically and emotionally, felt
shame, and tried to cover themselves with fig leaves. This didn't do the trick. Don't you know
God was thinking, *What is happening, you two?* Only God can cover our sin and shame.
We all have both and need His covering.

God killed an animal and made proper coverings for them with the animal skins. This
represents the first sacrifice. In God's holy design, blood atones for sin. Romans 6:23 (NIV)
says, "For the wages of sin is death, but the gift of God is eternal life in Christ Jesus our
Lord." He gives us a physical picture through this first sacrifice in Genesis of what is to come.
Sound familiar? God is always giving us visuals that we can understand.

In the Old Testament Jewish culture, they had an animal sacrificial system to atone for their
daily sins. This is known as the old covenant, and it existed before Christ came to earth.

Here's another verse that shows us how the old covenant worked: "For the life of a creature
is in the blood, and I have given it to you to make atonement for yourselves on the altar; it
is the blood that makes atonement for one's life" (Leviticus 17:11 NIV).

What this verse means is that those who are covered by the blood sacrifice are set free from the consequences of their sin. All the many blood sacrifices in the Old Testament foreshadow the ultimate blood sacrifice made by our Bridegroom, Christ.

Read Hebrews 9:11–18.

- What was Jesus's sacrifice on the cross a ransom for?

In the Old Testament and under the old covenant, God's people, the Jews, would sacrifice a lamb to cover sin. In John 1:29 (NIV) in the New Testament, Jesus was starting His earthly ministry, and John the Baptist called Him "the Lamb of God who takes away the sin of the world." Jesus came to fulfill the old covenant, and His mission was to shed His blood in the ultimate sacrifice on the cross to save us from our sin.

So how does this all tie in? Jesus's blood paid our bride price. He paid with the highest cost, His own life. He wants to cover our shame and cleanse us with His Spirit, and He asks us to receive His gift of eternal life. Just as Jack, the farmer in our story, wants to purchase Diane as his bride, Jesus already paid the price for us. We only have to accept His invitation.

He gave us His life to save ours. If that isn't true love, I don't know what is.

Day 3: Do You Take This Man?

Let's recap. The groom's father has chosen the bride. Jack and his father have presented the betrothal contract (the *ketubah*) to Diane and her family, and the bride price negotiations have been made. Now we're waiting on the bride-to-be's response. Will Diane say yes?

What I love about Jewish culture is that the woman had a choice. She had the right to choose. In this time period, this was not customary in other faiths. Women were seen more as property. God had set the Jewish people apart for His purposes starting in Genesis with Abraham. Abraham was Jewish, and he is the patriarch, or father, of our faith.

Through Abraham's seed comes the seed of Christ. Jesus was Jewish too. God gave the Jewish people the Ten Commandments through His chosen servant, Moses. God established the original Jewish law and laid a foundation of protection and justice for the Jewish people not found in other cultures of that day.

For example, God did not approve of polygamy, which was common then. As early as Genesis 2:24 (BSB), we see God's design for marriage. "For this reason a man will leave his father and mother and be united to his wife, and they will become one flesh." God says "wife" (singular), not "wives." As a rule, the ordinary Jew lived in a monogamous marriage. God protected women in this culture. They were provided for and taken care of by their husbands. They were under contract to acquire what they rightly deserved within the marriage. God showed us a model of what marriage should look like and gave the men and women their roles within the marriage.

Read Ephesians 5:25–33.

- How should husbands love their wives?

God gave a man and a woman distinctive roles in their marriage relationship, which gives us a visual picture of our relationship with Christ. We are to submit to Him, and He is to love us as His own body and lay down His life for us. This is a perfect picture of what Christ did for us on the cross.

There are many metaphors in the Bible used to describe a believer's relationship to Christ, but none are more visible and symbolic to the life of a Christian than the Jewish marriage ceremony process.

So what will Diane say? Let's look at the next step in the betrothal process. A cup filled with wine called the "cup of acceptance" would be presented to the bride-to-be. The bridegroom would drink half of the cup and then give it to the woman. If Diane drinks the other half of the wine out of the same cup, that would mean that she accepts the invitation and says yes!

Let's pretend she drinks the wine. She's all in. (It gets even better from here!)

The groom, Jack, would then shower her with gifts called the *mattan*. These gifts included jewelry, spices, oils, and even money. Girls! Again, who's going to help me bring these customs back? I'm counting on you all to spread the word. This is a thing.

After she says yes, Diane will wear a veil. This is kind of like how we wear an engagement ring today. The veil sets her apart from the other women in her village and lets everyone know that she is spoken for. Jack put a ring on it, okay, fellows?

Let's again take a look at the parallels we find in Scripture pertaining to us and Christ. When the Bible references drinking the cup, it's a sign of admission. It's like saying, "Yes, I accept." For example, let's look at various verses about accepting the mission and drinking the cup.

> My Father, if it be possible, let this cup pass from me; nevertheless, not as I will, but as you will. (Matthew 26:39b ESV)

> But Jesus said to them, "You do not know what you are asking. Are you able to drink the cup that I drink, or to be baptized with the baptism with which I am baptized?" (Mark 10:38 NASB)

> And he took a cup of wine and gave thanks to God for it. He gave it to them and said, "Each of you drink from it, for this is my blood, which confirms the covenant between God and his people. It is poured out as a sacrifice to forgive the sins of many." (Matthew 26:27–28 NLT)

And Jesus said to them, "The cup that I drink you will drink, and with the baptism with which I am baptized, you will be baptized." (Mark 10:39b ESV)

Jesus drank the cup. He was all in as our Bridegroom. Now He's offering it to us.

These verses are dripping with symbolism. When we drink the cup, we're saying yes and entering in. In this case, the bride is drinking the cup of her bridegroom and saying, "I'm bound to you. I will drink the cup of marriage and everything that includes. I will sign the contract. The suffering, the joy, the pain, the endurance, the sickness, and the health—the whole shebang!"

Spiritually, when we drink the cup of accepting Jesus as our Lord and Savior, His spirit enters us, and we are bound to Him for all eternity. Nothing can snatch us out of His hands. It's not based on works or anything we do, but on His grace alone. He has purchased us with His blood, and He immediately covers us from our sin.

Whether we feel anything or not, we are saved, and we become betrothed to Him. This is more than the *ketubah* we learned about the first day. This is a blood covenant. This contract is life and death, and all we have to do is say yes.

On another note, when we take communion at church, we're drinking the cup of acceptance with Him and remembering the lifelong covenant we made with Him. We're reminded that we are all in. We drink the cup of commitment to Jesus to share in this cup with Him and remind ourselves of our betrothal to Him, knowing in full faith that the wedding is coming!

Now, let's examine the parallels of the gifts, or *mattan*, we talked about above. When we accept Jesus, we receive the ultimate gift of His spirit, the Holy Spirit. Check out what Scripture says about this:

And Peter said to them, "Repent and be baptized every one of you in the name of Jesus Christ for the forgiveness of your sins, and you will receive the gift of the holy spirit. (Acts 2:38 ESV)

Now there are a variety of gifts, but the same Spirit; and there are varieties of service, but the same Lord; and there are varieties of activities, but it is the same God who empowers them all in everyone. To each is given the manifestation of the Spirit for the common good. (1 Corinthians 12:4-7 ESV)

Just as the Jewish bridegroom gave his bride the gift of marriage, he also showered her with his love by blessing her with special gifts of oil, jewelry, and other things personal to her. Jesus, our Bridegroom, gives us the gift of the Holy Spirit, which washes us clean, saves us from our sin, and makes us new. We then have eternal life and are forever connected to Him. Within this gift, His spirit gives us personal gifts to bring Him glory and spread His love all over the world.

Now let's examine parallels with the veil. Just as the woman would wear a veil to show that she was betrothed and set apart to be married, when we belong to Christ, we're set apart for Him. We belong to Him alone. Read the verses below:

You have been set apart as holy to the LORD your God, and he has chosen you from all the nations of the earth to be his own special treasure. (Deuteronomy 14:2 NLT)

Paul, a servant of Christ Jesus, called to be an apostle, set apart for the gospel of God, which he promised beforehand through his prophets in the holy Scriptures, concerning his Son, who was descended from David according to the flesh and was declared to be the Son of God in power according to the Spirit of holiness by his resurrection from the dead, Christ Jesus our Lord. (Romans 1:1–4 ESV)

Marriage is a physical picture of a spiritual reality. We'll all be married and become fully submitted to Christ in the heavenly realms. All believers, men and women, will be unified in perfect intimacy with Christ in heaven. We're not married in a sexual sense like we are here on earth; we'll be spiritual beings in a spiritual realm. Marriage gives us a picture we can understand to parallel the experience of perfect intimacy and unity in Christ in a spiritual form.

This is kind of deep stuff, isn't it? Tomorrow we'll pick back up on the wedding and honeymoon.

Just to keep us on our toes, I made a chart to cover the steps in the betrothal process. Let's fill in the blanks:

- First, the groom's father _____ the bride.

- Next, the groom's family visits the bride's family to offer a contract called a _____.

- The bridegroom and the bride's family then negotiate to determine the bride price and _____ the bride.

- The bride has a choice. If she chooses to say yes, she then drinks the _____ _____ _____.

- After she accepts, the contract is signed, and the groom showers her with gifts called _____.

- The bride is considered taken and will wear a _____ to set herself apart as spoken for.

Good job! Way to hang in there! Now let's get to the good stuff.

Today we're going to discuss the second phase of the Jewish wedding process, the marriage ceremony and feast. Let's begin with the honeymoon suite.

In Jewish culture, after the betrothal is finalized, the groom will spend the next year or so building a room for him and his bride. This is referred to as the "bridal chamber," which is kind of like a honeymoon suite. The bride and groom will not be allowed to see each other during this process.

Let's get back to Jack and Diane. Jack is now ready to build this bridal chamber at his father's home. It will be like an add-on room, so Jack and his bride, Diane, would have their own quarters and privacy. These rooms are always built in the home of the groom's father. This room will be the place where the marriage is consummated after the wedding ceremony is completed. Jack and Diane will spend seven days in the bridal chamber together, getting to know one another on an intimate level. The building process usually takes up to one year, and they will not be allowed to see each other or spend time together until this room is completed.

By the time the room is finally completed, Jack and Diane will have been apart for at least a year, longing for this time to finally be together. The building of the bridal chamber room is an intricate process, and Jack will take great pride in making it beautiful and wonderful for Diane. He'll stock the room with proper provisions for the two of them, knowing they'll be there together for seven days. It will be exquisite. Jack's father will be the overseer of the bridal chamber building process, and when his father feels the room is suitable and completed to his standard, he'll tell Jack to go get his bride.

Now during this building process, Diane will be watching and waiting for her husband, not knowing when the room will be complete, but knowing that it's in the works. No one, not even the son, knows the exact time the father will give him permission to go and get his bride. Diane will be making herself ready, knowing the time is coming. She definitely doesn't want to be caught unprepared! Being prepared includes watching for the signs of the readiness of the bridal chamber and making sure her wedding garments are clean and hung so as to not get wrinkled.

Let's apply this process to modern-day life. Girls, we know the grueling process of making ourselves ready for our weddings. We get in total beauty mode for months before our big day. If Diane lived in our day, she would be getting facials, losing weight, getting her hair highlighted, and having her nails done. You know it, girl. This is her big day. She would have the right shoes, dress, and makeup—the whole thing. She would be ready for her man to come and get her. This is our equivalent for how she would be "getting her wedding garments ready."

Okay, so Diane is getting ready and waiting for her big day. Jack is working to get the bridal chamber built and finalizing all the details. When Jack's father feels the bridal chamber has met his expectations, he'll give his son the command to go get his bride. This begins the next step in the Jewish wedding process, the procession.

The procession normally took place at midnight. It was kind of like a surprise attack. The groom would wait until the village had gone to sleep before gathering his friends. They would take oil lamps to illuminate the night and then march through the village blowing the trumpet and shouting, "The bridegroom comes!" This custom was a joyful experience for the whole community. Everyone would wake up and come outside to see the groom go and get his bride.

Jack is now ready to march to Diane's family's home. Hearing the trumpet and commotion, she'll be outside eagerly waiting for her bridegroom!

Let's apply this picture to our spiritual walk with Christ, beginning with the bridal chamber. "In my Father's house are many rooms. If it were not so, would I have told you that I go to prepare a place for you? And if I go and prepare a place for you, I will come again and will take you to myself, that where I am you may be also" (John 14:2–3 ESV).

In this passage, Jesus is preparing His disciples for His death and resurrection. Doesn't it sound familiar? He's going to His Father's house, and there isn't just one room, but many. Some interpretations even say "mansions," not rooms. We who belong to him have a place prepared for us. We'll have our very own bridal chamber, and it will be exquisite. These rooms or mansions represent the Father's personal preparations for us believers. We have a place in heaven prepared for us, and He's getting it ready.

Jesus wants to be with us and share in intimacy with us personally and as a body of believers. We belong. It isn't a sexual intimacy like we have here on earth. We're spiritual beings, and we'll share in the oneness of belonging to Christ as we become fully submitted to Him. We're not sure what that looks like in the spiritual realm, but we can be assured that it will exceed any feeling of bliss, pleasure, excitement, or wholeness that we've ever experienced in this life. We'll not only be—and already are—fully known by Christ, but we'll fully know Him too.

Let's read another verse that helps us understand the spiritual beings we become. "At the resurrection people will neither marry nor be given in marriage; they will be like the angels in heaven" (Matthew 22:30 NIV).

In other words, we marry Jesus and are joined to Christ, the head of the church, but we won't marry one another. That order will have passed away, and we'll have a better covenant—just as the Old Testament sacrificial system passed away and Christ became the new sacrifice. The old mirrored the new, just as our earthly marriage mirrors something new in the supernatural. We don't know exactly what is coming, but we do know that it will be far better than what we experience now.

Now let's look at the procession and see how that applies to us. Read the following verses:

> But about the day or hour no one knows, not even the angels in heaven, nor the Son, but only the Father. (Matthew 24:36 NIV)

> Then will appear in heaven the sign of the Son of Man, and then all the tribes of the earth will mourn, and they will see the Son of Man coming on the clouds of heaven with power and great glory. And he will send his angels with a loud trumpet call, and they will gather his elect from the four winds, from one end of heaven to the other. (Matthew 24:30–31 ESV)

> Behold! I tell you a mystery. We shall not all sleep, but we shall all be changed, in a moment, in the twinkling of an eye, at the last trumpet. For the trumpet will sound, and the dead will be raised imperishable, and we shall be changed. For this perishable body must put on the imperishable, and this mortal body must put on immortality. (1 Corinthians 15:51–53 ESV)

> At midnight the cry rang out: "Here's the bridegroom! Come out to meet him!" (Matthew 25:6 NIV)

Just as the Jewish groom sounds the trumpet and goes and gets his bride, Jesus will get the okay from His heavenly Father, the trumpet will sound, and Jesus will come and get us, His bride! This is called the rapture. The church, the bride of Christ, will be snatched out of this world and taken up to heaven with Jesus. Not even Jesus the Son knows when God the Father will give the final command, but we do know that like the bride in the Jewish wedding, we'll hear a trumpet sound, hear Him coming for His bride, and finally meet our Bridegroom face-to-face.

We also need to eagerly prepare for His arrival like the bride in the Jewish wedding prepared her garments. We need to make sure we're covered. So how do we know if we're wearing our wedding garments?

That's right! We accept Jesus's invitation to eternal life. His Spirit enters us, and we're covered in His robe of righteousness, which is the garment of salvation. Read the verses below and let's look at what the wedding garments represent for us as believers:

Let us rejoice and be glad and give him glory! For the wedding of the Lamb has come, and his bride has made herself ready. Fine linen [the righteous acts of God's holy people], bright and clean, was given her to wear." (Revelation 19:7 NIV)

We're clothed or covered by Christ when we belong to Him. He covers our shame and sin with robes of righteousness. We're made ready when we put our faith in Him and invite His spirit to come into our lives, make us pure, and cleanse us.

So where does this leave us? Jesus, our Bridegroom, is preparing a place for us. When the heavenly Father gives Jesus the Son the okay, Jesus will come and get His bride, which includes all believers or the universal church.

We'll hear the sound of the trumpet and then be taken up to meet Jesus in the air. This is the rapture, when all believers are taken out of the world to be with Christ, our Bridegroom. We'll put on immortality and prepare for our wedding to Him, the Lamb of God who takes away our sins and gives us eternal life.

Amazing stuff. Let's call it a day.

Day 5: I Now Pronounce You Husband and Wife

Jack and Diane are about to tie the knot. Before they say "I do," Diane needs to receive a ceremonial cleansing or ritual bath and then put on her wedding garments or dress. (FYI, I hate the word "garment.")

The bride has now made herself ready, and the bridegroom has her by his side. The bride and groom are ready for the wedding ceremony. She has on her linen wedding gown and veil, and they step into a *huppah*, a Hebrew word meaning "tent" or "covering." It looks like a canopy. Jack then presents the *ketubah*, the original contract, to his bride in the wedding ceremony. The ceremony would include Jack and Diane going under this canopy to exchange vows and rings, which is something we still do today.

The next step involves seven blessings that are recited over the bride and groom. Jack and Diane will select special guests to recite the blessings over them. After each blessing, the bride and groom will drink from a shared cup of wine symbolizing their union. Then the breaking of glass occurs, which is said to symbolize that joy must be tempered. It also represents the Jewish people's suffering over the destruction of the Jerusalem temple. The groom breaks a piece of glass by crushing it with his foot. Then the ceremony is complete, and the happy couple heads to the wedding chamber.

The married couple will now enter the bridal chamber and consummate the marriage. The consummation of marriage represents a blood covenant made between the husband and wife. Jack and Diane, our bride and groom, completed the ceremony and will spend seven days here together growing in intimacy and deeper understanding of one another. When they emerge after seven days, the feast begins!

In Jewish culture, there are many feasts held for celebrations, and this feast was held in celebration of the bride and groom. A wedding was a wonderful reason to celebrate! Everyone from the bride and groom's families and all the wedding guests will participate in eating wonderful food, drinking fine wine, dancing, and laughing to wonderful music. They'll tell family stories, share traditions, and grow in intimacy celebrating together. It's a marvelous party!

Let's read the following verses to learn more about how this relates to us:

But when the kindness and love of God our Savior appeared, he saved us, not because of righteous things we had done, but because of his mercy. He saved us through the washing of rebirth and renewal by the Holy Spirit, whom he poured out on us generously through Jesus Christ our Savior, so that, having been justified by his grace, we might become heirs having the hope of eternal life. (Titus 3:4–7 NIV)

"Come now, let us settle the matter," says the LORD. "Though your sins are like scarlet, they shall be as white as snow; though they are red as crimson, they shall be like wool." (Isaiah 1:18 NIV)

Isaac brought her into the tent of his mother Sarah, and he married Rebekah. So she became his wife, and he loved her; and Isaac was comforted after his mother's death. (Genesis 24:67 NIV)

"Let us rejoice and be glad and give the glory to Him, for the marriage of the Lamb has come and His bride has made herself ready." It was given to her to clothe herself in fine linen, bright and clean; for the fine linen is the righteous acts of the saints. Then he said to me, "Write, 'Blessed are those who are invited to the marriage supper of the Lamb.'" And he said to me, "These are true words of God." (Revelation 19:7–9 NASB)

Then I saw a new heaven and a new earth; for the first heaven and the first earth passed away, and there is no longer any sea. And I saw the holy city, new Jerusalem, coming down out of heaven from God, made ready as a bride adorned for her husband. And I heard a loud voice from the throne, saying, "Behold, the tabernacle of God is among men, and He will dwell among them, and they shall be His people, and God Himself will be among them, and He will wipe away every tear from their eyes; and there will no longer be any death; there will no longer be any death; there will be no longer be any mourning, or crying, or pain; the first things have passed away." (Revelation 21:1–4 NASB)

Now we see but a dim reflection as in a mirror; then we shall see face to face. Now I know in part; then I shall know fully, even as I am fully known. (1 Corinthians 13:12 BSB)

So how does this play into our relationship with Christ? We, like the bride, Diane, in this illustration, receive a ceremonial cleansing when we invite the Holy Spirit to dwell in our souls. We're washed clean and made new. The blood of Jesus covers us, and we're seen as righteous—pure as snow.

When we drink the cup of acceptance and say yes to Jesus, we become betrothed to Him. This is the first step in the wedding process. He chooses us, He purchases us with His blood, and we enter into an eternal contract that can never be broken. We are His. We're marked by Him in this life and set apart for His purposes. We belong to Him; He loves us.

We won't see Him face-to-face until we depart from this earth and enter into eternity, but we know that right now, He's preparing our rooms in His Father's house and He'll come back for us when the Father gives Him the command. He'll return for us with a loud trumpet call, and we will all meet Him in the air in the twinkling of an eye. We, His bride, are to be ready and eagerly awaiting and anticipating His arrival. No one knows the day or time when the bride will be summoned for the wedding.

The wedding to come will happen before Jesus's second coming. The wedding will happen right after we are raptured. He'll take His church, His bride, out of the world, and a time of tribulation will happen on earth. The second coming will mark the new heaven and earth that is prophesied in Revelation. We dive deeper into this topic in week six.

We are not sure when this prophecy will be fulfilled or when the rapture will take place, but what we do know is that the wedding of all weddings and party of all parties is coming. We want to be betrothed to Jesus and eagerly anticipate His return! We only have a picture, and we only understand in part, but one day we'll see it all clearly. Jesus is coming, and He is longing for the hour when He gets to marry His bride.

To wrap up this week, let's review the wedding process.

Part 1

- We're chosen: God the Father chooses us.
  - See Ephesians 1:4, John 15:16, Matthew 22:14, and Ephesians 2:19.
- We're purchased: Jesus paid the bride price with His blood.
  - See 1 Corinthians 6:20, Galatians 3:13–15, Colossians 1:13–14, and Acts 20:28.

- We take the cup of acceptance: We get a choice.
  - See Matthew 26:27.
- We receive gifts: He gives us the Holy Spirit and spiritual gifts.
  - See Acts 2:38 and 1 Corinthians 12:4–11.
- We wear a veil: Once we say yes, we're set apart.
  - See Deuteronomy 14:2 and Romans 1:1–4.
- We're ceremonially cleansed: The Holy Spirit washes us clean from sin.
  - See Titus 3:3–7.
- We're betrothed to Christ: We await His return.
  - See 2 Corinthians 11:2, Hosea 2:19, Ephesians 5:31, Hosea 2:20, and Matthew 1:18.

Part 2:

- He prepares the bridal chamber: Jesus is preparing our rooms/mansions for us.
  - See John 14:2–3.
- No one but Father knows when He will come: The trumpet will sound, and He'll come.
  - See Matthew 24:36 and Matthew 24:31.
- He arrives in the procession: Jesus comes for His bride in the rapture.
  - See 1 Corinthians 15:51–53 and Matthew 25:6.
- We celebrate the wedding with a feast: All believers will be married to Christ, fully submitted to Him for eternity. It's the party of a lifetime!
  - See Revelation 19:7–9, Revelation 21:1–4, and 1 Corinthians 13:12.

Group Guide

- Welcome the Group

- Open in Prayer

- Watch Week 1 video found at LaynieTravis.com/willyoumarryme (26:40)

- Go over discussion questions or as many as time allows for:
    1. What are the two main parts of the Jewish marriage process?
    2. What is a betrothal?
    3. What are some parallels between the Jewish wedding process and our walk with Christ?
    4. What does communion at church represent in the bridegroom context?
    5. How did Jesus purchase us as His bride?
    6. Once we accept His hand in marriage, how does our contract with Christ differ from the "ketubah" we learned about this week?
    7. How did the Jewish wedding process protect Jewish women in that day and age?
    8. When the bridegroom returns, where does he take his bride?
    9. How long are the bride and groom in the honeymoon suite?
    10. What are your thoughts on the future wedding and prophetic events we learned about this week?

- Close in Prayer

WEEK 2

Ready or Not

Day 1: The Ten Virgins

This week, we'll be examining two parables: one about ten virgins (sounds weird, I know) and the other about a wardrobe disaster (we can all relate to this one).

We're going to start this week off by talking about the parable of the ten virgins. It sounds kind of creepy, but trust me. After we look into it this week, you'll have a new perspective.

Read Matthew 25:1–13.

- Why were five of the virgins considered wise? What made the other five foolish?

Jesus often teaches in parables. Parables are stories with a moral or spiritual truth behind them. In this parable, Jesus is referring to the rapture. The word "rapture" refers to the final assumption of Christians into heaven during the end times. In other words, the rapture is when Jesus will return as our Bridegroom to take His bride, the universal church, out of this world to meet Him in the air. The procession of the Jewish bride that we learned about in week one is a picture of what this event will possibly look like.

Let's dive into this parable. I know this story sounds like a horror-movie title, but bear with me and you'll be pleasantly surprised.

The reason Jesus explains that the girls are virgins in this parable is to clarify that they were not yet married. Remember in week one when the bride was betrothed to her husband? They won't consummate the marriage until after the wedding ceremony. Before the ceremony, the groom will be busy building a bridal chamber in his father's house for his bride. He'll get the okay from his father when the room meets the father's standards, and then—and only then—will he go and get his "virgin" bride to officially marry her.

Jesus calls these girls "virgins" in this parable to clarify that they're not yet officially married. These virgins are most likely in the betrothal period waiting for their bridegroom to come and get them. It is not saying that you have to be a virgin in the sexual sense for Jesus to approve you as His bride. It's also not saying that if you've sinned, lusted, or fallen short in the sexual category, you're unqualified to be His bride.

This parable has nothing to do with our physical sexual status; rather, Jesus is using a physical example to explain a deeper spiritual truth. The fact that these girls are virgins mirrors how we're all spiritually in the virgin stage, awaiting a future marriage to Christ.

This parable can get a bad rap because we assume that it has to do with our physical purity. When we receive the gift of the Holy Spirit, we're made pure in Christ, meaning all of our sins are washed away and we're covered in robes of righteousness. We're saved from hell and become spiritually betrothed to Christ. Through the Holy Spirit, we receive our ceremonial cleansing once and for all. This isn't based on our works but on the blood of Jesus. We're covered in His blood and seen as pure in the eyes of God.

That being said, whether or not we're physically pure has nothing to do with this parable. It contains a higher spiritual meaning. These ten virgins represent people in the world today. We're all spiritual virgins waiting for the return of Jesus, our Bridegroom, to come and fetch us for the wedding that awaits us. Then we'll become one with Him in our glorified spiritual state and celebrate perfect unity in Christ.

Remember how five of these virgins were considered wise and five were not? Why is that? When we read verses 3–4, we learn that the five who were considered wise took extra oil with their lamps. The foolish five didn't take enough oil for their lamps. Let's read some more verses to understand why this is significant:

> You shall charge the sons of Israel, that they bring you clear oil of beaten olives for the light, to make a lamp burn continually. (Exodus 27:20 NASB)

> The responsibility of Eleazar the son of Aaron the priest is the oil for the light and the fragrant incense of the continual grain offering and the anointing oil—the responsibility of all the tabernacle and of all that is in it, with the sanctuary and its furnishings. (Numbers 4:16 NASB)

> Take also for yourself the finest spices: of flowing myrrh five hundred shekels, and of fragrant cinnamon half as much, two hundred and fifty, and of fragrant cane two hundred and fifty, and of cassia five hundred, according to the shekel of the sanctuary, and of olive oil a hin. You shall make of these a holy anointing oil, a perfume mixture, the work of a perfumer; it shall be a holy anointing oil. (Exodus 30:23–25 NASB)

Then you shall take the anointing oil and pour it on his head and anoint him. (Exodus 29:7 NASB)

The Spirit of the Lord GOD is upon me, because the LORD has anointed me to bring good news to the afflicted; He has sent me to bind up the brokenhearted, to proclaim liberty to captives and freedom to prisoners. (Isaiah 61:1 NASB)

These verses give us the context that oil was used in the Old Testament to anoint or set something apart, to make someone holy, and to consecrate a person or object to God. The oil is symbolic of the Holy Spirit. When we accept Jesus as our Lord and Savior, the Holy Spirit anoints us with His oil. And like the lamps in this parable, we have an oil that never runs dry.

Our lamps (our bodies) are lit up for God. We're wise, filled with the oil of His spirit, and rightfully betrothed to Christ, our Bridegroom. We're ready for His return.

Here's the bottom line: The virgins who have no oil are considered foolish and unprepared for His return. As a result, they're left behind. They represent those here on earth who have not received the Holy Spirit and are not yet betrothed to Christ.

The virgins who have oil represent the betrothed believers who are bound to Christ in this life. These believers have received the gift of His Holy Spirit and will be ready and considered pure when Jesus comes back for them.

Let's not forget our oil!

Day 2: Prepared

Over and over, we see references in Scripture to the return of Jesus being unexpected. Today we'll learn the importance of being prepared for it, even though no one knows the hour He'll come.

Read Matthew 25:6–9 (NIV).

- We see again in these verses that the bridegroom came at midnight and a cry rang out. "Here's the bridegroom! Come out to meet him!" Does this sound familiar?

In week one, we learned that in an ancient Jewish wedding procession, the groom would come to the bride's house at midnight with the sound of a trumpet. Once he arrived, she would wake up and quickly go out to meet him.

In this parable, the bridegroom also awakens the ten virgins. They all trim their lamps, but the foolish ones don't have the oil ready. The virgins with no oil attempt to take the oil from the ones who have it, but the ones with the oil wouldn't give it up. The foolish virgins were unprepared.

There's a lesson here: You can't receive the Holy Spirit by asking it of another person. It's a personal decision. Each of us as individuals has to accept the gift of salvation on our own. We're not saved because our parents, grandparents, or close friends are saved. We alone have to receive the gift of the Spirit (or the "oil," as the parable puts it) to receive salvation. Jesus offers each of us a personal invitation to be His bride.

Let's take a look at two scenarios to better understand what it means to be ready. Imagine you're going on a trip. Your flight leaves early in the morning, and you have to be at the airport early to not miss it.

Here's Scenario 1. It's the night before your early-morning flight. You haven't packed, and you know you should, but you can't get motivated to start. You decide you can just shower and pack in the morning. You stay up way too late watching Netflix. You forget to double-check the alarm you thought you set on your phone earlier in the day. Morning comes, and you awaken to a honk outside your house, followed by the doorbell ringing. It takes a minute before you realize what's happened. Then panic sets in. You've overslept!

This is the worst feeling, and I know because I've been there. You jump out of bed, your adrenaline is pumping, and you realize that the airport shuttle is at your house. You're not packed, you haven't showered, and we can't even talk about your hair. You wake up and try to accomplish your morning routine going 100 miles per hour, frantically brushing your teeth and hair at the same time, hoping there's no traffic, and praying that the airport shuttle guy sitting in the driveway will be willing to wait a little longer. You're bumping into things and knocking over your makeup pencils in a frenzy, trying to pack and get ready for a long trip in two minutes. (I'm sweating just thinking about this scenario!)

This is what the unprepared virgins in this parable would feel like. I know I don't just speak for myself when I say that I hate this scenario because I've overslept more often than I care to admit. And I've definitely been late to the airport. This gives us a picture of what it could possibly be like if we're not prepared when Jesus, our Bridegroom, comes back for us. He'll come at a time no one will expect, so we need to have our spiritual lives in order. We don't want to be caught sleeping and miss the plane!

Now let's look at Scenario 2. It's the night before the big trip. Your bags are packed and ready to go. You check in for your flight on your phone. You go to bed early, but before falling asleep, you double-check your alarm to make sure it's on and set at the right time. Your clothes and shoes are neatly laid out right by your bed, and your hair has been washed and blown dry to save a step in the morning. (Girls, I know you get this hair-already-done thing. Good hair is crucial in the good scenario plan.) You have your tote to carry on the plane by the front door with your favorite magazine, a fresh pack of gum, and your phone charger in the pocket. You wake up, only hit snooze once, make your coffee, get ready, and are looking out for the airport shuttle guy. When he arrives, you're more than ready. Can anybody say *wise virgin?*

I think we can all agree that the second scenario is a much better way to start a trip. So how can we be prepared for Jesus when He comes back to get His bride and not *miss the plane?*

We need to have the oil in our lamps by asking Jesus and the Holy Spirit to come dwell inside us. We then become believers and accept His invitation to marriage. By drinking this cup of acceptance, we can be assured that we belong to Him for all eternity and are ready for Him to return and take us to the wedding.

Then we stay awake spiritually and use the gifts He's given us to bring Him glory and be a light in our community. We shine our light for Jesus in this dark world. When He returns, He'll find us operating in our callings.

Read Hebrews 12:1–3.

- What do we need to "throw off" in order to run the race marked out for us?

- Where should we fix our eyes?

Jesus wants us to be fully running in the race He's marked out for us. If we do, when He returns, He'll find us pursuing Him and living for Him.

Read Matthew 24:1–8.

- What are some signs of the end times we need to watch for?

Jesus will come back for His bride. This is a promise. We can expect it. We want Him to find us prepared and walking out our callings. We want to be betrothed to Him, spiritually awake, and expecting His return.

Day 3: The Closed Door

Today, let's look at the last few verses in the parable of the ten virgins.

Read Matthew 25:10–13.

- Where did the virgins who were ready go?

- What did the bridegroom say to the five foolish virgins?

- Why should we keep watch?

As we just read, when the bridegroom arrived, the five foolish virgins weren't ready. They had no oil in their lamps, which we've interpreted to mean that they hadn't received the gift of the Holy Spirit. They were unprepared, and as a result, they didn't make it to the wedding. The door was closed.

It's kind of like the plane in the first scenario yesterday. Once the door is shut, it won't open—no matter how much you beg and plead.

Let's read some more verses to give us more context on closed doors in Scripture, starting in Genesis with the story of Noah and the ark. It took Noah a hundred years to build this ark, and the door was open until it wasn't.

> You are to make a roof, finishing the sides of the ark to within eighteen inches of the roof. You are to put a door in the side of the ark. Make it with lower, middle, and upper decks. (Genesis 6:16 CSB)

> The animals going in were male and female of every living thing, as God had commanded Noah. Then the LORD shut him in. (Genesis 7:16 NIV)

> As it was in the days of Noah, so it will be at the coming of the Son of Man. For in the days before the flood, people were eating and drinking, marrying and giving in marriage, up to the day Noah entered the ark. (Matthew 24:37–38 NIV)

Just as the ark had only one door to pass through to escape God's judgment, we too have only one door to escape God's judgement. His name is Jesus. By faith, Noah and his family entered into the ark. Once they were inside with their families and the animals, God shut the door. The door is open to us, and the invitation is open to all who say yes. Let's say yes and walk through the door of salvation because time is short!

What else does the Bible have to say about doors?

> I am the door. If anyone enters in by me, he will be saved. (John 10:9a WEB)

> Behold, I have set before you an open door, which no one is able to shut. I know that you have but little power, and yet you have kept my word and have not denied my name. (Revelation 3:8b ESV)

> What I mean, brothers and sisters, is that the time is short. (1 Corinthians 7:29a NIV)

> Behold, I stand at the door and knock. If anyone hears my voice and opens the door, I will come in to him and eat with him, and he with me. (Revelation 3:20 ESV)

I love that last verse. Jesus knocks on the door of our heart. Our Bridegroom wants to come in, dine with us, and be a part of our lives. When we shut Him out, we're actually shutting ourselves out of eternity with Him.

Let's take a look at one last verse today. "Ask, and it will be given to you; seek, and you will find; knock, and it will be opened to you" (Matthew 7:7 ESV).

There's a time when the door will be opened, and that time is now. Jesus wants us to let Him in. When we knock on His door and seek to find Him, he joyfully and thankfully opens the door to us. There will come a time when it will be too late, and when we knock, the door will not open.

Let this be a warning to let Him in now so we won't find ourselves like the foolish virgins who don't get to come and be a part of the wedding. We'll never know the day or hour, so we must have the door open and ready.

Day 4: Fear of Being Invited

One of my closest friends was telling me that she doesn't have fear of missing out (FOMO). She has fear of being invited (FOBI). I thought this was so funny!

I get FOMO when I see a group pic on Insta that I'm not included in, but she's just the opposite. She told me that when she gets an invite in the mail, a sense of dread comes over her, and she thinks, *Oh no. What do I have to go to now?* We laughed, but I tell this story as an illustration of the next parable we're about to read. Let's check it out.

Read Matthew 22:1–14.

- According to verse 14, how many are invited?

- How many are chosen?

Let's examine this parable. In the first line, we see that the king is giving a banquet for his son. Remember, we now have a historical understanding of the father-and-son relationship pertaining to the wedding customs of the day. The men of the family are in charge of throwing the wedding feast party.

The father, who is the king in this parable, then sends out his servants to call those who have been invited to the wedding feast. With the king throwing the party, you know it's going to be amazing!

What happens in verses 3–6 when the servants go to call the people who had been invited to the party? Can you believe it? They don't come! It's the party of the year with all the best décor, choicest foods, finest wines, most breathtaking music, and dancing—all free of charge—and the people in the community snub the king. They experience FOBI. They don't want to be included.

They not only don't go, but they also kill the servants who come to generously invite them to the party. We might all have a little FOBI, but none of us would ever think of going this far, right? This is crazy town. I can't get my head around this! The king in the parable can't understand this logic and cruelty either. What is his reaction, and what does he do?

We see in verses 7–10 that he's of course enraged! He then avenges the death of his innocent servants by sending armies to destroy the murderers and set their city on fire. He was sharing all he had with his so-called friends and community, and they not only rejected him, but they also murdered his servants!

This would be like getting a personal invitation to attend the royal wedding and hang out and feast with Queen Elizabeth and Duchesses Kate and Meghan and then not only rejecting the invite but murdering the invitees. Can you imagine not attending the royal wedding of Meghan Markle and Prince Harry? That alone is unheard of. I watched that amazing wedding over and over on my device, and to get to go in person would be surreal!

The king decides that those who rejected the invite aren't worthy to come. He then resolves to have his servants invite people outside his social circle and community. They go to the streets and highways and invite everyone they come across, both good and evil alike, and they're able to fill the banquet hall with unlikely guests who gladly accepted the invitation.

What do you think is the meaning of this parable? Let's examine two interpretations.

First Interpretation

God chose the Jewish people through father Abraham to carry the seed of Jesus, His Son and our Savior. Jesus was Jewish and born through a Jewish lineage in the line of Judah. When Jesus came on the scene, He wasn't what the Jewish people expected. They expected a warrior, and He came as a suffering servant. He came in power, but it looked different than what they had believed.

Most of the Jewish people didn't accept Jesus to be the Savior, and in doing this, they rejected the Father's plan: that in order to come to the Father, you must go through Jesus, His one and only Son. They were God's chosen people and lived under the law of Moses given to them by God. They were invited, but many have rejected the new covenant that's present in the New Testament.

Read Romans 11:11–31.

- According to verse 14, what did the Jews' rejection bring to the rest of the world?

- What does it mean to be "grafted" into God's family?

So the first spiritual interpretation of this parable is this: The Jews are the people in the parable who were invited first to the wedding. They're God's chosen people. He chose them and set them apart. Jesus wants them as His bride, but when they rejected God the Father's plan, God then went to other highways outside the Jewish people and extended the invitation to the Gentiles.

Now, the Gentiles—those who aren't Jewish—are grafted into God's family when we accept His invitation. We get to come to the wedding! God used this part of the plan to include us all. In His sovereignty, He was always going to include us. We'll see how the story plays out for eternity. He loves the Jews and Gentiles alike. He calls us all to be His bride, and the choice is up to us.

Let's read one more verse to understand this concept. "There is neither Jew nor Gentile, neither slave nor free, nor is there male and female, for you are all one in Christ Jesus" (Galatians 3:28 NIV).

Now under the new covenant, there is no Jew or Gentile, but only those who believe in Christ as Lord and those who do not. It does not matter what your denomination, gender, background, race, family, or social status is. Only one thing matters: You either believe Jesus is Lord and accept His invitation to eternal life, or you reject Him.

Regardless of the church you attend and the works you've done, if you don't take the invitation given to you, then you won't get to attend the wedding feast and be married to Christ. This is a serious matter!

Second Interpretation

Let's start by reading these verses:

> He does not want anyone to be destroyed, but wants everyone to repent. (2 Peter 3:9b NLT)

> The Spirit and the bride say, "Come!" And let the one who hears say, "Come!" Let the one who is thirsty come; and let the one who wishes to take the free gift of the water of life. (Revelation 22:17 NIV)

This parable also applies to all people living now on earth. The king in this parable represents God the Father, the son represents Jesus, and the wedding feast refers to those God invites now into salvation.

Those who reject God the Father's invitation to the great wedding celebration of eternal life in Christ will become like the subjects in this parable, burned and killed. The consequence of their rejection will be an eternal death. This is and never was God's will for us. He's inclusive and longs for everyone to come!

Let's not be foolish and reject the good news and free gift of salvation. Those of us who are saved will participate in an actual future wedding. Anyone who hears the gospel receives the invitation to come to the wedding feast of the king, so we're all invited. We just have to RSVP that we accept and are coming. Will you accept the invitation?

Day 5: Wardrobe Malfunction

Have you ever had that dream where you show up to a party without your shoes or in your pajamas? It usually goes something like this: You're at a party, and you're not sure how you got there. Then suddenly you realize that you're in your PJs or you don't have any shoes on. All of your friends are there in their Sunday best, and you're unprepared, underdressed, or maybe not even dressed at all! You're fully exposed, and everyone is staring and laughing. As far as bad dreams go, these fall into the nightmare category in my book. I always wake up horrified and then breathe a sigh of relief that is was only a dream.

I've had this dream more times than I can count. I also have the dream where my teeth fall out. Do I need therapy? Maybe. Okay, let's move on to the last portion of this parable.

Read Matthew 22:11–14.

- What was the king's response to the man without proper wedding clothes?

- Why do you think the kind had the man bound and thrown out?

This seems like kind of a cruel reaction by the king. However, it does hold important biblical truths. God takes this stuff seriously. He loves us and wants us to know that our choice here is a matter of life and death. He's warning us that apart from His grace and forgiveness, we're headed for destruction! Both this parable and the parable of the ten virgins have graphic consequences when we don't choose Him. He isn't sugarcoating this. Let's dig in.

Read Revelation 19:6–9.

- What is the bride wearing, and what does it represent?

This verse explains that those who are in Christ are clothed with fine linen bright and clean. We're made new, and our sins are forgiven and washed away. He covers us, and we're like a bride made ready.

In this culture, kings would often provide wedding attire for the guests to put on at royal wedding feasts. To refuse to wear these provided clothes would be a sign of defiance and disrespect to the king. Imagine being invited to the royal wedding in England for Prince

Harry and the beautiful Meghan Markle and then wearing your workout gear with old crusty tennis shoes. Maybe you show up sweaty with dirt on your face and no lipstick on. (I look like death with no lipstick, so that alone would be enough to draw negative attention!)

It would be like you were making a point to stand out and show your disapproval of the entire event. It would be offensive and bring shame upon the event. By refusing to wear the proper clothes, the man in this parable was being defiant and bringing dishonor upon both the wedding and host. He was aligning himself with those who had rejected the invitation and making a point of showing disrespect to the king.

When the king personally confronted his behavior, the man was rendered speechless. The majesty and holiness of the king's presence was more than he could bear. He couldn't stand up under the scrutiny of the king's gaze.

The man was then thrown out. The king's pronouncement in Matthew 22:13 (ESV) is chilling. "Bind him hand and foot, and cast him into the outer darkness. In that place there will be weeping and gnashing of teeth."

I don't ever want to go to that place. I'll gladly wear my garment. The point to take away from this parable is that God takes sin seriously. Evil, darkness, and the horrible hurt and pain of sin and injustice in this fallen world all need severe consequences.

For justice to be served, sin has to be reconciled. There has to be a standard of righteousness, and there has to be punishment for the darkness and evil of sin. Jesus took that punishment for us on the cross. Through His sacrifice, He saves us, covers us, and reconciles us unto God. This is grace, people. Why would we reject His offer of grace, love, and eternal joy and bliss? Why would we throw that back in His face?

When sin is unaccounted for, the punishment is severe and includes death and eternal separation from God. In our sinful nature, we simply can't stand up under the scrutiny of God. He is holy, and apart from Him, we are not. The man without proper wedding attire tried to make a mockery of God, and God will not be mocked.

Let's reread the final verse of this parable, along with another verse I'm sure you've heard before.

> For many are called, but few are chosen. (Matthew 22:14 ESV)

> For God so loved the world that he gave his one and only Son, that whoever believes in him shall not perish but have eternal life. (John 3:16 NIV)

So who is chosen? Those who are truly committed. They choose to come, they drop everything to come, and nothing can hold them back from getting right with God. They get it. They'll pay any price, make any sacrifice, and do anything to be with Jesus because they know their sins need saving.

Jesus came and died for us so we can have eternal life in Him. If we thought the royal wedding in England was grand, we'll be amazed at the wedding put on by God Himself. When we give our lives to Jesus, we can be confident that we'll be at the wedding of the Lamb and the banquet held by the true king, God the Father. We'll be ready.

Group Guide

- Welcome the Group

- Open in Prayer

- Watch Week 2 video found at LaynieTravis.com/willyoumarryme (25:27)

- Go over discussion questions or as many as time allows for:
  1. What is a parable?
  2. Read Matthew 25:1–13. Why were the girls called "virgins"?
  3. Why were five of the virgins considered wise? Why were five considered foolish?
  4. Read Revelation 19:7. How do we "make ourselves ready" for Christ in this life?
  5. What happened when the five unprepared virgins tried to borrow some oil from those who had enough? How does this relate to us today?
  6. Where did the virgins who were ready go? What did the bridegroom say to the five foolish virgins?
  7. Read Matthew 22:1–14. According to verse 14, how many are invited? How many are chosen?
  8. What is the response of the first round of invitees to the banquet thrown by the king? What did the king do as a result?
  9. Read Galatians 3:28. What do you think is the meaning of this verse in light of what we learned this week?
  10. Why do you think the man in the parable chose not to wear the wedding garments to the wedding? What were his consequences?

- Close in Prayer

The Bride, the Groom, and the Well

Day 1: Want to Grab a Drink?

Well, y'all, we made it to week three. This week, we'll look at two patriarchs of our faith, Isaac and Jacob. They were both Jewish and married to Jewish women, which means they would have undergone the Jewish marital customs of the day. We'll see evidence of the wedding process we learned about in week one throughout both of their stories.

Both Isaac and Jacob found their future wives at a water well. When studying the Bible, you'll find that when something happens more than once, it's not a coincidence. Moses, another patriarch of the faith, also met his wife at a well, and in future weeks, we'll learn that Jesus met the Samaritan woman at a well. Let's take a look at wells today and see why this meeting place is significant.

In biblical times, wells were usually located outside of town and required a one- to two-mile walk to get to them. They often served as boundary lines to mark that a village was close by. Women of the village would take two or more trips to the well each day to gather water for their family's daily needs, such as drinking, washing, agriculture, and cooking. Wells were a crucial life source for a community in that day.

A functioning well that was full of water was not only a necessary and life-giving source for a community. It was also a social hub, kind of like Starbucks is to us today. (I need coffee like I need water. Just saying.) Travelers would come from near and far to drink water and refresh their animals. The well, being just far enough outside of town, was an acceptable place for young men and women to meet, visit, and flirt (just keeping it real) outside of the watchful eye of their elders. You could often find a shepherd hanging out around midday or evening time resting and watering his flock before heading back on the road.

Water in the Bible symbolizes life. In the book of John, Jesus refers to the Holy Spirit as "living water." The Holy Spirit brings eternal, supernatural life. An empty well in the Bible is referred to as a "pit," a symbol of death with no life-giving source or water dwelling inside. Pits were empty, dark, dry, and deadly.

Check out this verse. "You are a garden fountain, a well of flowing water streaming down from Lebanon" (Song of Songs 4:15 NIV).

King Solomon spoke of his bride as a well flowing with streaming water. When we, the bride of Christ, have the Holy Spirit dwelling inside us, we're like the well that King Solomon describes in this verse. It's truly a beautiful picture. Being "like a well" was considered a great compliment in this culture. It implies that you're refreshing and life-giving, and all who come in contact with you are filled with life.

Wells were also a common place for betrothal scenes in the Bible. Weddings then were commonly held at the community wells. The well is present at each betrothal meeting that we'll look at this week. Wells can also be referred to as "springs" in certain Bible interpretations.

Today let's read the two stories below. Then we'll spend the next couple of days breaking them down. It's a lot of reading today, but trust me. They're romantic and set the precedent for what we'll be studying. Read Genesis 24:1–67 and Genesis 29:1–20

I told you they were romantic! Hang on tight. Tomorrow is even better.

Day 2: She Says Yes

There's so much amazing history found in the story of Isaac and his betrothal to Rebekah. We can really see the Jewish wedding customs at play here. Let's reread the verses below, keeping in mind all that we've learned about this process.

Read Genesis 24:1–16.

First, we see that Isaac's father wanted to choose a bride for Isaac. Remember this from week one? The father chooses the bride for his son. Next, we see that the father sends his servant to Abraham's own country among his Jewish relatives to find a Jewish bride for Isaac. His servant is extremely prayerful, asking God to show him the right woman for Isaac.

Rebekah was the daughter of Bethual, son of Milcah, who was the wife of Abraham's brother Nahor. She was Jewish and a distant relative of Abraham. She was said to be very beautiful and a virgin. The servant spotted her by the well, and she immediately offered him a drink of water from her water jar. God made her the obvious choice and clearly answered the servant's prayer.

How does the Lord make it clear that Rebekah is the right choice? She not only gave him a drink, but she went on to water all ten of his camels. This girl was a total overachiever!

Just FYI: To appreciate the full gravity of this task, it's important to note that camels drink a lot. One camel can drink fifty-three gallons of water in three minutes. It could have amounted to 530 gallons of water to satisfy these thirsty camels, so this would have required a lot of work on her part going back and forth gathering water for them. This was a true act of sacrifice.

She served a man she didn't know with no idea that he was looking for a wife for his master's son. She served him wholeheartedly and went above and beyond without expecting anything in return. We see so much of her amazing character revealed in the way she treated a stranger.

I can assure you that based on this evaluation, I would not have been chosen. I get stranger danger; plus camels scare me. I don't want to be near them, and I especially don't want to gather 530 gallons of water for them. (I'm not what you would call an animal lover. I like them and think they're cute, but I don't want to pet them. They smell. Okay, moving on.)

In verses 33–50, we see the servant of Abraham making the bridal arrangements for Rebekah by approaching her family and explaining the unique situation of his role. He came as a representative of Abraham and was responsible for choosing a bride for his master's son, Isaac. He clearly was a trusted member of their household. He then goes on to discuss the *ketubah*, or wedding contract, with Rebekah and her family. In this discussion, they cover the bride price we learned about in Week 1.

Read Genesis 24:51–53.

• What does Abraham's servant give Rebekah and her family?

Exactly. The servant offers her the *mattan*, the wedding gifts she receives from him after she accepts the offer.

Aren't you glad we studied the customs in week one? It really does give us a whole new appreciation and understanding of the Jewish wedding process.

Read Genesis 24:54–61.

• Did Rebekah have a choice in this process?

Yes, and she accepted! Due to the unique situation of the servant being the representative, she and the groom weren't able to drink the cup of acceptance to affirm her choice then, but I wanted to remind you of this step in the customary process.

Let's now look at the many parallels between this bride, Rebekah, and the bride of Christ. In this nonfiction Bible story, we're reminded that the father chooses the bride just as our heavenly Father chooses us. Jesus will return for a pure bride made new in Him.

This servant chose Rebekah, just as God the Father chooses us. Rebekah, the chosen bride, was found to be faithful right where she was, going above and beyond in service. Her heart was pure, and God blessed her for her great servant heart and hospitality. Let this be a reminder to us all to remain faithful to God our Father right where we are. We never know when a divine assignment is on its way.

The servant found her at a well, which we learned yesterday was a popular betrothal and wedding spot in Jewish culture and holds rich symbolism of life. He then paid a bride price for her, just as Jesus paid a price for us by dying on the cross for our sins.

Rebekah had the choice to become betrothed to Isaac, a man she had not yet seen. As believers, we haven't yet seen Christ, but we choose Him by faith and become betrothed to Him when we say yes. Finally the servant showered Rebekah and her family with gifts, just as Jesus gives us the gift of His Spirit and covers us with a garment of salvation.

Isn't the symbolism God gives us in this story so amazing? There are so many parallels between this betrothal and our relationship with Christ. I'm a visual learner, so I love how the Lord gives us glimpses throughout His Word that apply to our spiritual life in Him.

Day 3: Isaac and Rebekah Tie the Knot

Let me catch you up to speed. Isaac and Rebekah have not yet been formally introduced. They're betrothed (or as we would say, "engaged") to be married, but they've never met. Talk about a leap of faith! I'd at least be asking a few minor questions to the servant guy before I said yes: How tall is he? How old is he? Does he have hair? Does he work out? Call me vain, but we all know she had to be curious as to what Isaac looked like.

Let's read on. "Now Isaac had come from Beer Lahai Roi, for he was living in the Negev" (Genesis 24:62 NIV).

Beer Lahai Roi was a well between Kadesh and Bared on the road leading to Egypt, so Isaac too was at a well. The name Beer Lahai Roi means "the well of the living one who sees me." God saw Isaac and his need for this bride.

God is a living God who sees our needs and knows what's best for us. It isn't a coincidence that the Bible mentions that the servant found Rebekah at a well and Isaac came from a well to meet her. God designed them for one another.

Read Genesis 24:63–67.

- What was Isaac doing when he first saw Rebekah?

- What did Rebekah do when she first heard that Isaac was the servant's master?

I love these verses. It reminds me of a scene in the film *Pride and Prejudice* where Elizabeth Bennet goes out into a beautiful field, and there's Mr. Darcy walking toward her at twilight. He's wearing a long man coat with longish hair, and their eyes meet as they continue walking toward each other. I love that movie, and that scene is beyond romantic. If you haven't seen it, please rent it today. You're welcome.

In the verses above, we read that Isaac left the well and was going to meditate in a field when he saw camels coming his way from a distance. Rebekah lifted up her eyes, and when she saw Isaac, she dismounted the camel. (Okay, ladies. I'm thinking he's a hottie.)

She asked the servant, "Who is that man?"

The servant answered, "He is my master."

Rebekah then covered her face with the veil. Remember how women would wear a veil when they were spoken for? I love it when the pieces come together. The servant then went ahead of her to meet Isaac and tell him all that happened. I'm sure he essentially bragged on Rebekah and was thrilled that he had more than delivered on Abraham's request.

Let's switch gears now and read a passage written by King Solomon to his bride. I can't help but think that it paints a beautiful picture of what Isaac could have been thinking when he first met Rebekah. It's a wonderful representation of the romance embedded into this Jewish culture and the promise that love and romance are so much sweeter when you wait on God's perfect timing.

Read Song of Songs 4:1–15.

- Which of these compliments is your favorite?

Solomon's seductive words of anticipation and desire for his bride as she hides behind her veil can still make a girl blush. He eagerly awaits their time together on their wedding night. Who says the Bible is boring? This is racy stuff, people!

Back in Genesis, we see the second part of Isaac and Rebekah's wedding process. If you remember, this includes the marriage and the consummation. Isaac had just lost his mother, Sarah, and he was grieving. God, in His perfect timing, comforted Isaac by bringing him his bride during this time of loss. The Bible says that Isaac brought Rebekah into his mother's tent.

Remember, the bride and groom would stand under a tent called a *huppah* to exchange wedding vows. The Bible goes on to say that Isaac loved Rebekah. I love this. He didn't just marry her to reproduce or to have a woman in his life after losing his mother. He really loved her. He cared for her. He desired her. He wanted her.

I love the way Solomon's love for his bride is described here. "He brought me to the banqueting house, and his banner over me was love" (Song of Songs 2:4 ESV). This gives us a beautiful picture of Christ's love for His bride. He's proud of us, and He shows the world like a banner flying high that we belong to Him. He loves us and proclaims His love for us like a flag over a nation. His banner, His slogan, and His mark over us is His love.

Just as Isaac brought Rebekah into his tent and loved her, Jesus brings us in and loves us too. We become part of His family when we're betrothed to Him. What was the spiritual meaning of a biblical tent? Let's read a couple of passages to learn more: Exodus 33:7–11 and Hebrews 9:1–15.

In the Old Testament, when God gave Moses the Ten Commandments at Mt. Sinai, He also gave him instructions for making a sacred tent of meeting known as the "tabernacle." This tent was to be Israel's place of worship. The people could gather in the front part of the tent, but only the priests could go into the inner part of the tent, which was separated by a curtain and known as the "Holy Place."

There was a second curtain that only the high priest could enter once a year to offer a blood sacrifice to God. This place was called the "Holy of Holies" or "Most Holy Place" because God's glory rested there and no man could stand in His presence and survive without first being ceremonially cleansed.

The "Most Holy Place" housed the ark of the covenant, a golden chest that held the Ten Commandments; a gold jar filled with manna; and Aaron's walking stick. The lid on this chest was called "the mercy seat" and represented God's throne on earth. It was the place where God's glory dwelled.

In the New Testament, Jesus came as our high priest, and through His blood sacrifice on the cross, the curtain that separated the "Most Holy Place" was torn, symbolizing that we can now enter into God's presence on earth because Jesus makes us clean.

When we accept Jesus's invitation to marriage, His Spirit comes to dwell inside us. In other words, we become the sacred tent of meeting. One day when He returns, we'll step into the tent of His kingdom to be joined to Him in marriage for eternity.

Day 4: Love at First Sight

Are you sick of love yet? I didn't think so. We're women. We love love!

Well, here goes love story number two. This is the second story we read on day one regarding Rachel and Jacob. Jacob is one of Isaac and Rebekah's twin sons. His love story is unique, and it isn't a coincidence that, like his father, Jacob also met his bride at a well.

Let's review by rereading the first part of this story. Read Genesis 29:1–6.

- What was covering the mouth of the well?

- What did the shepherds need to do to access the water?

We have a few of the same characters in this story. Laban in this story has a daughter named Rachel, and as we saw in the story of Isaac and Rebekah, he's also Rebekah's brother. He'll soon become Jacob's father-in-law. This is quickly becoming a small-town scenario where everyone knows everyone and they're all becoming relatives.

We see some similar parallels in the love story between Rebekah and Isaac and that of Rachel and Jacob. For starters, Isaac and Jacob both travel from a distant land, and both find their future wives at a well.

I love how this story is set up. Jacob is coming from a distant land and is weary from his travels. It's midday, and he stops at a well to grab a drink of water and refresh. He runs into several local shepherds at the well and begins to socialize with them and do some name-dropping.

While he's talking to the shepherds, he sees a beautiful young woman approaching with her sheep. He turns on his charm. Jacob has got some game! Look what he says next.

Read Genesis 29:7–10.

- What did Rachel do for a living?

Jacob's trying to get the shepherds that are currently at the well to take their flocks and leave. He tells them that this isn't a good time for them to be at the well. He tells them to water the sheep and go pasture them. He's essentially saying, "Get outta here! A pretty girl is approaching, and I want her to myself. Give me some space to do my thing."

They don't get the hint. When Rachel arrives with her father's sheep, the shepherds are at the well watching them. Rachel was a shepherdess, and the Bible says that she was beautiful. Jacob is instantly enamored with her. He immediately rolls the large stone from over the mouth of the well away and waters her flock of sheep for her. I can't help but think he was like his mother, Rebekah. The overachieving gene must have run in the family! Rebekah has watered ten camels, and Jacob is now watering all of Rachel's flock. They were servant types, and I bet their love language was acts of service. (Just saying.)

Read Genesis 29:11–14.

- What did Jacob do after he watered his uncle's sheep?

Yep, you read it right. Jacob laid one on her! Well, to be fair, it was customary in this culture to kiss as a greeting, so he was being politically correct. However, you know he was dying to kiss her. The Bible says he wept when he greeted her, which reveals so much about his personality. He was open with his expression of feelings and vulnerable with her. I love that he was a passionate man who didn't hold back.

Rachel then runs and tells her father that a relative of theirs was at the well, and Laban runs to greet him. Then he invites him to stay for a month. I can't help but wonder: What did Rachel think of him?

Let's take this story so far and apply it to our lives spiritually. I love that Jacob immediately wanted Rachel to himself. He saw her, and he liked what he saw. Jacob is a prototype of Christ and patriarch of our faith. Jesus sees us and is in love with what he sees. Jesus wants us and wants time alone with us. Just as Jacob removed the stone so Rachel could access the water in the well, Jesus rolled the stone away from His tomb and rose from death so we could access the living water of His Holy Spirit.

Let's learn more by taking a look at these passages: Luke 24:1–8, John 4:14, and Ezekiel 36:26.

Jesus gives us water from a well that never runs dry. Our sin is like the stone that covered this well. It blocks our access to the living water. Jesus removed the stone of our sin and offers us eternal life and direct access to the Father.

Jesus also serves us, His bride, just as Jacob served Rachel. He not only gives us living water, but also uses us to water our flocks, just as Jacob offered water to Rachel and her sheep. God makes us a shepherd over people in our lives. Like Rachel, you have people to shepherd, whether you're a mom with children, a teacher with students, a doctor with patients, or an encourager to friends in your circle. God will water you and then use you to refresh others spiritually.

Finally Jesus wants intimacy with us. Just as Jacob kissed Rachel and wept, Jesus also rejoices and grieves with us. He holds nothing back from us, and He wants vulnerability in our relationship with Him. He desires to know us and be known by us. Just as Jacob was enamored with Rachel, Jesus is enamored with you. He loves you and thinks you're beautiful and marvelous. He saves you, and He saves me.

Through Christ, the stone of sin that covered our hearts is rolled away, and we have full access to God. He died so we can live!

Day 5: The In-Laws

If you think you have dysfunctional relatives, let's read this and all feel better about our family situations. If your in-laws are worse than this, I suggest therapy—lots of therapy!

Read Genesis 29:15–30.

- How many years did Jacob originally offer to work for Laban?

- How many years did he end up working for him in order to marry Rachel?

The veil (and possibly being overserved at the banquet) totally tripped Jacob up. He ended up marrying Leah, Rachel's older sister, thinking it was Rachel. Wowza! Laban, his father-in-law, put her up to this and totally tricked Jacob.

Now, remember in the first week when we learned that if you couldn't pay a bride price to purchase your bride, another option would include working for the bride? Well, that's exactly what's happening here. This story doesn't include all the steps we've covered in the Jewish wedding process, but we do get glimpses of the negotiations along the way.

The Bible says that the first seven years flew by because of his love for her. He was head over heels for this girl.

By the way, did you notice that he completed the week with Leah? This is in reference to their time together in the bridal chamber spending a week together in intimacy. But what happens after he completes his week with Leah?

You got it: He'll finally get to marry Rachel, but he'll still have to work for Laban for seven more years. He works fourteen long years for this girl to earn her. It's super romantic, but it's also so cruel for Leah.

He's married to sisters! I have two sisters, and we don't even like to share clothes. I can't imagine what these girls went through having to share a husband! It's weird, gross, and complicated. This is a nightmare for everyone involved.

These are real problems, and I don't want to just brush over the Leah dilemma. The Lord provides for her and meets her in her troubles just to reassure you. He blesses her with four sons. God helps her and meets her in her pain. I love that God can make good out of anything.

Let's look now at the parallels and see how the story of Rachel and Jacob applies to us as the bride of Christ today.

Just as Jacob willingly worked for Rachel for fourteen years, Jesus is relentless in His pursuit of us to win us as His bride. He works for our hearts and will continue to chase after us, wanting us for His own. He pursues us, and He already gave us everything. He came down from heaven and died a sinner's death to pay for our sins—all in the name of love for us, His bride.

Check out this amazing image of how far Christ, the Good Shepherd, will go for us:

> Suppose one of you has a hundred sheep and loses one of them. Doesn't he leave the ninety-nine in the open country and go after the lost sheep until he finds it? And when he finds it, he joyfully puts it on his shoulders and goes home. Then he calls his friends and neighbors together and says, "Rejoice with me; I have found my lost sheep." (Luke 15:4–6 NIV)

Jesus will never give up in His pursuit of you. He wants us, but there is an enemy—a Laban—in each of our lives who desperately wants to confuse us and thwart God's plans. Our spiritual enemy, Satan, wants to keep us from our marriage to Christ. He wants to deceive us and trip us up to make us feel unlovable and unworthy, but Christ will always fight for us. He'll never stop pursuing us.

Let's close this week with this thought: Rebekah and Rachel both came to a well, a source of water and life, and there they found their husbands. They were chosen as brides by men who loved them individually and uniquely. They were known, prayed for, sought after, served, loved, desired, and chosen—just as you are known, prayed for, sought after, served, loved, desired, and chosen by Jesus.

When we come to the well of the living water of Christ and drink the cup of acceptance, we meet our Bridegroom, Jesus, and become His bride.

Group Guide

- Welcome the Group

- Open in Prayer

- Watch Week 3 video found at LaynieTravis.com/willyoumarryme (33:33)

- Go over discussion questions or as many as time allows for:

    1. What do wells represent in the Bible?
    2. Where did several patriarchs of our faith meet their wives?
    3. How did Isaac's servant know that Rebekah was God's choice for him?
    4. What did Abraham's servant give Rebekah and her family? Did Rebekah have a choice in the betrothal process?
    5. What are some parallels between Isaac and Rebekah's story and your own story with Christ?
    6. Read Song of Songs 4:1–15 as if Christ were saying these things to you. Which of these compliments is your favorite?
    7. What did Jacob see as he was traveling on a journey? Whose daughter did Jacob see approaching the well as he was talking with the shepherds?
    8. What did Jacob do after he watered his uncle's sheep?
    9. How many years did Jacob originally work for Laban? How many years did he end up working in order to marry Rachel? Why did he work for Rachel?
    10. What are some parallels between Rachel and Jacob's story and our walk with Christ?

- Close in Prayer

Never the Bridesmaid, Always the Bride

Day 1: Han Solo

Weddings are magical. No matter who's getting married, there's something sacred and fairy tale-like about the whole wedding experience. As special and wonderful as weddings are, we've all been the single person at one. When I was in my early twenties and had just graduated from college, I was literally in twelve weddings. I had a variety of bridesmaid dresses and interesting hair updos captured in pictures for years to come. Thank goodness we didn't have Instagram back then!

As much as I loved the honor of playing a special part in each of my close friends' weddings, my dream of my own wedding was always in the back of my mind. Although I was always happy for the bride, I couldn't help but look forward to the day when I would be the bride.

Jesus understands this longing. He put this desire in our hearts before time began. Whether we're married or single in this present world, when we say yes to Him, we become His bride and belong to Him for eternity.

Read John 2:1–12.

- What was happening in these verses in Cana?

- Who is mentioned being at this wedding besides Jesus and His disciples?

Many scholars believe that because Jesus, His mother Mary, and His brothers were all present at this wedding, it was quite possibly a relative of Jesus that was getting married. At this time, Jesus lived in Nazareth, and Cana was located 8.3 miles away in Galilee from Nazareth. Jesus had not yet performed any signs or wonders. He had been baptized by His cousin John, had chosen His disciples, and was now attending a community wedding (quite possibly a family wedding) in Cana.

Just to give you context, in any culture it would be embarrassing to run out of wine at a wedding. Much like weddings today, in the Jewish community, weddings were a reflection on the family hosting them and took a great deal of intricate planning. If the host ran out of wine in this culture, not only would it be an embarrassment, but it would also bring shame upon the family. It even violated the Jewish laws of hospitality.

If this were indeed a family member's wedding, then we can assume that Mary would have been somewhat involved in the planning process. She even seems to take responsibility for the wine dilemma. She informs Jesus that the wine had run out, and knowing who Jesus is, she desperately relies on His help to save her family from shame.

What does Jesus say to His mother when she tells Him they're out of wine? (Reread John 2:4 NIV for the answer.)

This seems sort of cold, doesn't it? For starters, He calls her "woman." I'd be so mad if one of my kids called me that. He goes on to say, "Why do you involve me? My hour has not yet come."

Let's focus on the "my hour" part of this sentence by taking a look at a few other verses in John:

> At this they tried to seize him, but no one laid a hand on him, because his hour had not yet come. (John 7:30 NIV)

> He spoke these words while teaching in the temple courts near the place where the offerings were put. Yet no one seized him, because his hour had not yet come. (John 8:20 NIV)

> It was just before the Passover Festival. Jesus knew that the hour had come for him to leave this world and go to the Father. Having loved his own who were in the world, he loved them to the end. (John 13:1 NIV)

> After Jesus said this, he looked toward heaven and prayed: "Father, the hour has come. Glorify your Son, that your Son may glorify you." (John 17:1 NIV)

In these verses, you see that when Jesus says "my hour," He's referring to His death and resurrection. He came to this earth to complete a mission to save us from our sins so we can spend eternity with Him. His "hour" is in reference to His coming crucifixion and resurrection.

Why does this matter? Well, there are a lot of reasons scholars believe that Jesus answers His mother's request in this manner. Let's focus on two interpretations that will help us see this from the Bridegroom angle.

When Jesus told His mother that His hour had not yet come, He was looking ahead and seeing the bigger picture. Sure, he could have fixed the immediate dilemma of the wine mishap, but He couldn't yet cover people's shame for good. His mission hadn't yet been completed. It was not yet finished. In fact, it was only just beginning.

His mission was, however, completed when He died on the cross and rose from the grave. Through His sacrifice, He defeated death, took the punishment for our sin, and covered our shame for good. However, at this point in Jesus's earthly ministry, the hour for the Son of Man to be glorified had not yet come.

Take a look at this verse. "When he had received the drink, Jesus said, 'It is finished.' With that, he bowed his head and gave up his spirit" (John 19:30 NIV).

Jesus says, "It is finished." In other words, the hour of His death had finally come, and now He would be glorified.

Let's go one step further and look at the second meaning of "the hour" he is referring to. When Jesus tells Mary that His hour hasn't yet come, He's also talking about a future wedding that awaits us. He's saying that the hour hasn't come for Him, our Bridegroom, to marry us, His bride.

I think this is where the disgruntled single guy comes into play. When Jesus's mother asks Him to get involved in this wedding, it seems to strike a personal nerve within Him. In that moment, I believe Jesus was reminded that He was the single guy at the wedding. He was Han Solo. Jesus was surely frustrated and even panic-stricken with this scenario because, after all, He's the one wanting and longing for the hour when He'll marry His bride. He wants us. He's waiting for us. A wedding and feast are coming, and they'll be the celebration of a lifetime!

At this point in the story, Jesus wasn't even in the betrothal stage with His bride. We couldn't yet be engaged because His ministry hadn't yet fully begun. I think it's fair to assume that He felt jealousy and heartache for His bride. Trust me. The hour of our wedding will come, and the Bridegroom won't just be attending as a bystander or working miracles behind the scenes. He'll be the Lord of the Feast, the King of Kings, and the one and only Bridegroom getting married to the love of His life. And that, my friend, is you.

Note: Information in today's devotional is referenced from Timothy Keller's sermon "A Wedding Party Encounters Jesus." Be sure to check it out online if you'd like to learn more on this topic.

Day 2: Party Foul

Ready for day two of the wedding at Cana? So far, there's a party, and the wine has run out. In today's terms, this would definitely fall into the "party foul" category. As we learned yesterday, this would not only be an embarrassment to the family hosting the wedding, but it would also bring horrible shame on them and even violate Jewish hospitality laws.

Read John 2:5–9.

- How much water did the stone water pots hold?

The servants filled the six water pots to the brim. That's a lot of water. They immediately and fully obeyed Jesus's orders because they trusted Him. Mary trusted Him too. He held an authority that people responded to. We don't see Mary or the servants doubting Him. Even with His odd response to Mary, she trusted that He could and would fix the problem.

When Jesus asks something of us as His servants, let's be obedient like the servants in this story. Let's obey Him to the full measure of our ability and fill our pots to the brim. There's always blessing in obedience.

At this time, water that was stored in water pots was not considered ceremonially clean unless it was stored in stone pots. So this was pure water that had been examined thoroughly and stored for ceremonial use.

After the servants filled the pots, the Bible says that they drew some out and gave it to the master of the banquet to taste. He then tasted the water (now turned to wine), and in his delight, he called the bridegroom.

This miraculous event reveals God's glory. He's showing His disciples who He is. Only God can change water into wine. This is a supernatural occurrence.

To understand more about the significance of this miracle, let's take a look at a few more passages in Scripture.

Read Exodus 7:17.

- When Moses is sent to deliver the Israelites from slavery, what's the first miraculous plague that God performs through him?

Read Exodus 4:25.

- What type of bridegroom does Zipporah say Moses is to her?

Sorry for the graphic verse here, but it's important to note that Moses is a prototype of Christ. In the Old Testament, God revealed the law (also known as the Ten Commandments) through Moses to the Israelites. The Ten Commandments represent the old covenant, or the law. The water turning to blood represents the sacrificial system in that there had to be blood shed to atone for sin.

Along with the animal sacrifices in the Old Testament, Jewish men had to be physically circumcised. This was an outward sign that they belonged to God. Jesus came to fulfill the old covenant and replace it with a better covenant of grace. He gave us many external pictures of what would be a future internal work.

Let's take a look at the following verses together: John 1:17, Deuteronomy 30:6, and Matthew 26:28–29.

The outward circumcision has turned internal. Now through the blood of Christ, our hearts can be circumcised. This was accomplished by Jesus shedding His blood for our sin on the cross.

Because of His sacrifice, we're now under a new covenant of grace. We're washed clean from sin once and for all, and He gives us a new heart. We now have direct access to God the Father, and we have the Holy Spirit dwelling inside of us. When we drink the cup of acceptance or the "wine" of the Holy Spirit, we become betrothed to Christ. A future marriage awaits us.

Jesus tells His disciples after the Last Supper that He won't share a cup of wine with them again until He's at the wedding feast. Remember, the bride and groom share a cup of wine at the wedding ceremony to seal their vows. Jesus offers us a cup, and when we drink the cup of acceptance to become betrothed to marry Him, we belong to Him in this life, we're filled with His spirit, and we're forever connected with Him.

Then one day we'll share a cup of wine with Him again at our wedding ceremony. We'll become joined to Him in marriage and become fully and wholly submitted to Christ, our husband. That's when we'll reach the fulfillment of our love relationship with Jesus.

Ellicott's Bible Commentary says it like this, "Never afterwards while he tarried upon earth was He to taste of the wine cup with His disciples. But in the kingdom of God, completed and perfected, He would be with them once again, and then Master and disciples would be alike sharers in that joy in the Holy Ghost, of which wine—new wine—was the appropriate symbol."

Let's read another verse that shows the spiritual metaphor of wine. "And no one pours new wine into old wineskins. Otherwise, the wine will burst the skins, and both the wine and the wineskins will be ruined. No, they pour new wine into new wineskins" (Mark 2:22 NIV).

This represents the new wine of the new covenant. It's a fulfillment or extension of the old. It's better. Jesus gives us the new wine of His spirit. The old wine represents the old sacrificial system and the law. Now we have the living water, or "new wine," which is the spirit of Jesus poured out on all who will drink of Him.

When Jesus ascended into heaven after defeating death, He sat down at the right hand of God the Father and then poured out His spirit on all mankind. He already drank His portion of the cup, and now He's asking us if we'll drink the new wine of the Holy Spirit and enter into a marriage covenant with Him.

When we drink this cup of His spirit, we accept His offer and are betrothed to Him for all eternity. His spirit takes up residence inside of us, and we're then set apart as His bride.

Let's read the following verses and dive more into the concept of the spirit of God being poured out onto us: Mark 1:8, Joel 2:28–29, 1 Corinthians 12:13, and John 3:34.

See the pictures He's painting for us in these visual examples? He pours out His spirit for us to drink. This is just like the cup of acceptance in the Jewish wedding ceremony.

Like a well that never runs dry or a party that never runs out of wine (the best wine), Jesus gives in abundance. He gives us exceedingly and abundantly more than we can ask, think, or imagine. He gives Himself to us fully and completely, and He wants us to give our lives to Him in return. He wants a mutual love relationship with us.

The God of the universe wants to be your bridegroom. Drink Him in.

Day 3: Drop the Mic

Jesus is the man. No, literally. He's not just a guest at this wedding; He's Lord of the banquet.

He comes to the wedding, saves the party, doesn't draw attention to Himself at all, saves this family from public humiliation (which only the disciples, Mary, and the servants know about), and makes the wine better than ever. Let's just say "Boom!" His job is done here. Drop the mic.

He saves this family from shame, brings joy and feasting, and keeps the party going. This is what He does for our lives as well. Wine in the Bible is a symbol of abundance, joy, and celebration. Jesus wants us to enjoy our lives. He came not to just give us life, but life to the full. He has good in store for us. He's our Bridegroom, and He wants to celebrate with us, His beloved bride.

Read John 2:9–11.

- Why was the master of the banquet surprised?

- Why do you think Jesus chose this as His first public miracle?

The bridegroom of this wedding got the glory, but behind the scenes, Jesus was showing His disciples that He's the one in charge. He's the true Bridegroom and Lord of the banquet. He alone provides the best wine for us, which we learned yesterday is His spirit.

In that day, the master of the banquet would be the father of the bridegroom, and he would be in charge of the great feast that took place after the wedding ceremony. Jesus is proving in this miracle that at this party—and in the party of life, so to speak—He's our true provider and He provides more than we could ask, think, or imagine.

Check out these passages on the great feast awaiting us: Isaiah 25:6–8, Luke 14:15, and Revelation 19:6–9.

Jesus is both our Bridegroom and master of the banquet now in this life and in the coming wedding and feast. He's in charge, and for those of us who accept His invitation, we can expect a party like none we've ever experienced.

Let's switch gears for a moment and look at a couple of passages from Song of Songs, written by King Solomon: Song of Songs 4:10–11 and Song of Songs 5:10–16.

In this book, King Solomon is describing his love relationship with his bride. This story also gives us a picture of our love relationship with Christ. Now let's get something straight because I know you're wondering. In that first passage, Solomon is not saying that his sister is his bride. (Gross.) "Sister" in Hebrew is an affectionate term often used for one's bride. Glad we got that cleared up!

He's saying that his love for her and her love for him are better than wine, just as Jesus's love for us is better than any substance we have access to here on earth. His love exceeds our expectations, as did the new wine served at the wedding.

In the second passage, Solomon's bride is describing his appearance. Who else does this appearance remind you of? I'm not sure if this is theologically accurate, but I can't help but picture Jesus, our Bridegroom, looking something like this on our wedding day.

Here's another picture of Jesus at His second coming. "I saw heaven standing open and there before me was a white horse, whose rider is called Faithful and True. With justice he judges and wages war" (Revelation 19:11 NIV). Jesus is fierce, mighty, powerful, majestic, and a true warrior. Words fail to describe Him in all His glory.

Imagine how humble Jesus was in His earthly body. When we get a glimpse of who He really is, we can appreciate His frustration in knowing that the time had not yet come for Him to reveal His full glory. The full story of the Bible still isn't finished. We're still here, and there's so much to come. He longs to reveal Himself in His glorified form to us.

The glorified, majestic, beautiful, strong yet gentle, and loving Jesus is coming back for us. We are His beloved, and He's the master of the banquet and our Bridegroom. I'd say that's definitely worthy of dropping the mic.

Day 4: Washed Clean

Let's look into these water pots today. Here's what we know: "Nearby stood six stone water jars, the kind used by the Jews for ceremonial washing, each holding from twenty to thirty gallons" (John 2:6 NIV).

In the verses following, Jesus tells the servants to fill the six stone water pots with water.

- What do you think is the significance of the presence of water and water pots at this wedding?

The Jews used these stone water pots for ceremonial washing. In this culture, the Jewish people would wash their hands before and after meals, and if this failed to happen, it was considered a transgression. Being ceremonially clean was a must to obey Jewish law.

The water stored in the stone pots was pure and preserved for the cleansing. These pots were large and held twenty to thirty gallons of water each. Jesus told the servants to fill the pots with water, and the servants obeyed and filled the pots to the brim. It's important to note that the pots were completely filled to the brim; no other substance would have fit into them. They were filled with water alone.

- Based on what we've learned about the old and new covenants, why do you think it was symbolic that Jesus chose the pure cleansing water in these ceremonial jars to be turned to wine?

This miracle foreshadows that the people would no longer need the outward washing of water to be ceremonially clean, just as they would no longer need the outward circumcision. (However, I still recommend this procedure!)

Jesus sent His spirit—also called the "living water"—after His mission on earth was completed, and we can receive an inward cleansing from our sin. By turning this ceremonial water into new wine, He gave a picture of the new covenant to come. The outward cleansing would no longer be necessary for spiritual purity.

It's no coincidence that the water in these ceremonial pots was the water He used to do His first miracle. He was giving a visual picture of what was to come: the old system becoming new. The water used in the old system for cleansing became obsolete when the living water of His spirit came. Jesus did all the cleansing through His sacrifice.

How does this new method of cleansing compare to the old method? Take a look at this verse. "Blind Pharisee! First clean the inside of the cup and dish, and then the outside also will be clean" (Matthew 23:26 NIV).

The old water only cleans only the outside and can't wash away our sins. The new wine of the new covenant foreshadowed in this story cleans us from the inside out, once and for all.

After the pots were filled, Jesus tells the servants to draw some water out and take it to the head waiter. They do what He asks, and when the head waiter tastes the wine, he mentions that everyone usually brings out the best wine first and saves the cheap wine until after the guests have had too much to drink, but they had saved the best until now.

As believers, we're betrothed to Christ here on earth and look forward to our future marriage and wedding feast. What the head waiter said is still true for us today. "The best is yet to come."

Jesus's disciples saw this miracle, understood that it was supernatural, and put their faith in Him. When we put our faith in Jesus, we become clean on the inside, we're made pure by His blood, and He washes our sins away.

He makes all things new, and the best is still yet to come!

Day 5: First Miracle

In the last day of this week's study, let's talk about why Jesus chose a wedding as the venue for His first miracle.

God created and blesses marriage. Marriage is a model for us of what it's like to be united with Christ. Jesus desires for us to have a love relationship with Him. It's a reciprocating love like the love between a husband and his wife. When we're eternally bound to Jesus, it will be a perfect, harmonious union—one of life and love and eternal bliss.

It doesn't matter if you're married or single in our life here on earth. Spiritually, we're designed to be united with Christ in perfect intimacy. He fulfills every relational need we have here on earth. We're complete in Him alone.

It's no coincidence that Jesus chose a wedding to demonstrate His first miracle. There's great significance in Him knowing that the hour for Him to marry His bride has not yet come. Again, He's hinting to us that there is a great wedding coming. He's telling us that He's the master of the banquet and our beloved Bridegroom and that you are not the bridesmaid. You, my dear—yes, you—are His bride.

When Jesus looks at you, He sees beauty, love, affection, desire, power, and holiness. He made you lovely, and you will be (and already are) loved and fought for to the point of death. He waits for you in His kingdom and can't wait to celebrate with you. You're worth it to Him.

Through this miracle, Jesus shows us what He came to bring: the joy, grace, and new wine of His spirit. He washes away our sin and covers our shame. When we drink the cup He offers us, He gives us His spirit without limit. He's with you, and He's in you. He has circumcised your heart and dressed you in fine linen. He sets you apart.

When you accept His invitation by drinking the cup of acceptance, He makes you His own and will come back to marry you. He saves the best for last, just as he did with the wine at this wedding. We can't even comprehend what's coming, but what we do know is that He is good and we want a seat at His table.

Take a look at this verse: "Taste and see that the LORD is good; blessed is the one who takes refuge in him" (Psalm 34:8 NIV).

Take a moment right now to reflect on His goodness. He's knocking on the door of your heart. He's down on one knee, asking for you to enter into this love relationship with Him. Only He can fill the hole in your heart. When you say yes, you'll be filled with His spirit, living water, and new wine. You'll forever be His bride.

Here's how you can say yes:

> Place me like a seal over your heart, like a seal on your arm; for love is as strong as death, its jealousy unyielding as the grave. It burns like blazing fire, like a mighty flame. Many waters cannot quench love; rivers cannot sweep it away. If one were to give all the wealth of one's house for love, it would be utterly scorned. (Song of Songs 8:6–7 NIV)

> Here I am! I stand at the door and knock. If anyone hears my voice and opens the door, I will come in and eat with that person, and they with me. (Revelation 3:20 NIV)

God is jealous for you, and His true love cannot be quenched. He wants you all to Himself. He wants you set apart for Him and His highest purposes for you.

Open the door of your heart to Him today. He wants to come in and dine with you. He desires fellowship with you. Just say yes!

Group Guide

- Welcome the Group

- Open in Prayer

- Watch Week 4 video found at LaynieTravis.com/willyoumarryme (26:15)

- Go over discussion questions or as many as time allows for:

    1. Read John 2:1–12. What was happening in Cana in these verses? Who is mentioned being at the wedding besides Jesus and His disciples?
    2. What does Jesus say to His mother when she tells Him that they're out of wine?
    3. Read John 7:30. What is Jesus referring to when He talks about His "hour"?
    4. Reread John 2:4. What is another interpretation of the "hour" Jesus refers to in this passage?
    5. How much water did the stone pots at the wedding hold? What happened to the water?
    6. Read Exodus 7:17 and Exodus 4:25. What is the first miracle plague that God performs through Moses? What type of bridegroom does Moses's wife Zipporah say he is to her?
    7. Why was the master of the wedding banquet surprised? Why do you think Jesus chose this as His first public miracle?
    8. What are some things that wine symbolizes in the Bible?
    9. Based on what you learned this week about the Old Covenant and New Covenant, why do you think it was symbolic for Jesus to turn the pure cleansing water in the ceremonial jars into wine?
    10. How does drinking the "new wine" of Jesus's spirit relate to the cup of acceptance we learned about in Week 1?

- Close in Prayer

A Match Made in Heaven

Day 1: The Cup of Acceptance

Well, y'all, we've made it to week five. This is probably my favorite week yet. It's full of rich symbolism and fascinating parallels. I can hardly wait to get started! Let's go.

Read John 4:1–6.

- Which well did Jesus sit by to take a break from His long journey?

It's no coincidence that Jesus sat down to talk with the Samaritan woman at the same well where Jacob would have met his bride, Rachel. As we saw in past weeks, wells were a common betrothal scene for the patriarchs of our faith.

Read Exodus 2:15–21.

- Where did Moses first meet his bride?

That's right. We see in this story that Moses also met his bride, Zipporah, at a well, just as Isaac and Jacob did. Let's read on in the story of Jesus and the woman from Samaria.

Read John 4:7–9.

- What did Jesus ask of the Samaritan woman?

In this culture, the Jewish people and the Samaritan people were enemies. By sharing a cup with a Samaritan, a Jewish person would actually become ceremonially unclean. What Jesus was asking this woman to do would've been considered completely countercultural. The Jews and Samaritans were not permitted to speak to one another, much less share a cup.

On another note, she was a woman. For a man to speak to a woman he didn't know in public was most unusual and greatly frowned upon. This intimate exchange between Jesus and this woman would be deemed inappropriate and socially awkward. Let's take a deeper look at what Jesus was really asking her.

You may be wondering: Where were the disciples in this story? This was just Jesus and the woman. They were alone, setting the stage for a private conversation.

Looking back to week one when we studied the Jewish marriage process, do you remember how a Jewish woman would accept a man's proposal to enter into a betrothal? We keep seeing this running theme: A cup of wine would be poured for them to share. If she agreed to the terms of the *ketubah*, she would drink the cup of acceptance.

Do you see it? Jesus and the Samaritan woman are alone at a betrothal scene—the same one as other patriarchs of our faith—and Jesus is asking her to share a cup with Him. I think it's safe to assume that He's inviting her into a marriage contract.

Read John 4:10.

- Based on Jesus's response, did the Samaritan really understand whom she was speaking to?

She's, of course, thrown off. She's confused by why this man is even talking to her at all, much less why he's asking her for a drink. He tells her that if she only knew the gift of God and who was asking her for a drink, then she would've asked Him for living water, and He would've given it to her.

So what does this mean exactly? He's offering her to share a cup of something infinitely better than the well water: His living water! This is the same living water that was foreshadowed at the wedding in Cana when Jesus turned the ceremonial water into wine. It's a vivid description of His spirit that was coming soon.

Let's break this down. If she decides to drink the cup of acceptance, then He'll give her a gift, and it will exceed her expectations. Here, the gift would be His living water.

He was essentially offering her a marriage contract in eternity! He was also demonstrating the model of salvation to us. He pours out His spirit (the living water), we drink it (by saying yes), and we become washed clean and forever betrothed to Him.

Don't miss this: In this interaction, Jesus is clearly inviting the Gentiles into His plan for salvation. We're all included—the Jew and the Gentile alike—and all we have to do is accept His invitation and receive the gift of His spirit. He came from the Jews, but the Gentiles are engrafted into this plan. All of us are invited to be His bride.

The fact that Jesus, the Bridegroom, is asking this Samaritan woman to share a cup is more than significant. She's a symbol of what His church will look like: people from all tribes and nations. He paid the bride price for all of us with His blood, and when we drink of the living water of His spirit, we become set apart for Him. We belong to Him.

Let's read more about this invitation.

> For there is no difference between Jew and Gentile—the same Lord is Lord of all and richly blesses all who call on him, for, "Everyone who calls on the name of the Lord will be saved." (Romans 10:12–13 NIV)

Amazing stuff, huh?

Day 2: Living Water

Yesterday, we saw Jesus starting up a conversation with the Samaritan woman by asking her for a drink. He was willing to share a cup with her. He told her that if she only knew who it was that asked her for a drink, then she would've asked Him for living water, and he would have given it to her. It was a wedding proposal.

What does living water represent? Let's read on in the story.

Read John 4:10–15.

- What does Jesus say is the difference between the well water and His living water?

- What is the Samaritan woman's response?

As we saw yesterday, Jesus was sharing the key to salvation with the Samaritan woman. She was a Gentile, so this is huge. Jesus was Jewish, and the Jewish people were God's chosen people. God chose them as His own and set up the law, the prophets, and the old covenant through them. Through the seed of Abraham came Christ, God's one and only Son. However, in this significant encounter at Jacob's well, we see Jesus opening the door of salvation to the Gentiles as well. They too are His bride.

Jesus is telling this Samaritan how to become betrothed to Him. If she asks Him for His gift of living water and drinks of it, then she'll never thirst spiritually. She too will be like a well of water that springs up to eternal life.

Let's take a look at another passage in John that illustrates this.

> Now on the last day, the great day of the feast, Jesus stood and cried out, saying, "If anyone is thirsty, let him come to Me and drink. He who believes in Me, as the Scripture said, 'From his innermost being will flow rivers of living water.'" But this He spoke of the Spirit, whom those who believed in Him were to receive; for the Spirit was not yet given, because Jesus was not yet glorified. (John 7:37–39 NASB)

In this passage, we see again that a feast is coming and in order for Him to send His spirit to us, Jesus had to be glorified. At this point in John, He had not yet been crucified and had not yet ascended into heaven.

Once the ascension took place and He sat down at the right hand of God the Father, then and only then, He poured out His spirit on all who would drink the cup of salvation. There was a divine sequence to these spiritual events.

The following passages give us more insight into Jesus's ascension and outpouring of His spirit: Acts 1:6–11, Mark 16:19, and Acts 2:17.

We're in a period called the Church Age where the Lord has poured out His spirit. The Holy Spirit is now available to any who will receive Him. Now just like at the wedding in Cana, we are to drink in His spirit that He poured out for us, His bride.

When we drink in His spirit and accept the cup of living water He offers, we're born again, making us new and alive in Christ. His spirit comes and takes up residence in us, we're saved from our sins, and we're betrothed to Christ for all eternity. This is a spiritual occurrence.

Let's take a look at verse 15 of our story again. "The woman said to him, 'Sir, give me this water so that I won't get thirsty and have to keep coming here to draw water'" (John 4:15 NIV).

She's saying, "I love this news!" She still doesn't fully understand the spiritual meaning behind Jesus's living water because she's taking His words literally. I love that she says she wants the water so she doesn't have to keep coming to the well because, whether or not she realizes it, that also carries a spiritual meaning.

The Jews had to continually perform sacrifices at the tabernacle so their sin could be atoned for, and only the high priest could enter into the Holy of Holies to communicate with God. The high priest would intercede on behalf of the people. In other words, under the old covenant, the people had to keep "coming to the well," or keep doing the works required, to get to God.

With Jesus's living water in the new covenant, we don't have to do works anymore. It's a new system based on grace. Jesus took our punishment, and as a result, we now have direct access to Him. No one has to go on our behalf. We don't have to "go to the well" and draw from the water of works or religion because we have the living water dwelling inside of us. Jesus is with us and in us at all times.

For the Samaritan woman, the trips to the spiritual well are now unnecessary. She's now the well that can hold the water of the spirit of Jesus. She's learning how to be filled spiritually and become the bride of Christ. All she has to do is ask for it.

Day 3: It's Complicated

Ready to pick back up on the story of Jesus and the Samaritan woman?

Read John 4:16–19.

- What is the Samaritan woman's current relationship status?

Okay, we can see that this woman has a complicated love life. I want to point out that her relational reality is dysfunctional. We don't know what all has happened, but we can probably all agree that love has failed her. She's gone from relationship to relationship and come up dry.

With her reputation with men, she would've definitely been looked down upon in her society (and even in our society today). I know women who are ostracized or looked down upon based upon their relational failures. We live in a fallen sinful world. This isn't heaven, and people aren't perfect. They mess up, and life and love are painful.

You can bet that this woman had been through an enormous amount of pain and brokenness. We know that she had a past of five husbands and was living with a man that wasn't her husband when she spoke with Jesus. She would've most definitely carried shame and heartache. She probably felt not good enough, not worthy of love, and like a failure. And it sounds like she may have given up on the idea of marriage.

Let's look at how good God is to her and to us. He meets us in our brokenness and doesn't heap judgment upon us, but He shows us the way to freedom and restoration. He gives this woman the keys to unending love. He invites her into an eternal marriage.

He offers her His hand and essentially says, "I can see that you've given up, but please don't lose heart. I'm going to blow your mind. I love you, and I want you. My love will not run dry. I'll satisfy the scorched places in your heart. I'll bind up the wounds and heal the broken places within you. I'll bring you love that lasts and new life that's full of joy. I want you as my bride."

This week is for those of us who have ever found ourselves in the same boat as the Samaritan woman. Maybe you're in a loveless marriage, your husband left you (or you left him), you're single and can't find someone to share your life with, or you're divorced and it was awful and messy and you feel like a failure. Whatever your situation, God's love covers it. His love doesn't run out. He's faithful.

Jesus knows your story just like He knew this woman's story, and He doesn't give up on you. You're worth it to Him. It doesn't matter if you're married or single, divorced or widowed, or with someone or alone. It doesn't matter where you stand here in your bodily form. The bottom line is that He wants you as His bride. He's holding out for you! He's saying to you, "Trust me! I'll never leave you or forsake you. I promise that if you ask me, I'll fill you, and I want to fill you. I want you!"

You can't out-sin God's grace. He loves you no matter what. He is love. He covers our shame and leads us to healing. He has big plans for your life.

Take a moment to read the following verses and experience God's comfort in your heart: Hebrews 4:16, Psalm 73:23–26, Jeremiah 29:11, and Isaiah 41:10.

Let's get back to the Samaritan woman. Jesus didn't rebuke or judge her based on her marital status. He revealed to her how to be spiritually right with Him. He showed her the keys to His kingdom and filled the longing in her soul. He loved her.

Let's wrap up by taking a look at a couple of passages that demonstrate God's unfailing love for us: Romans 5:8 and Ephesians 5:25–32.

Know this today: The Samaritan woman is who Jesus came for, and so are you.

Day 4: The Hour Has Come!

Let's start today by going back to Jesus's first miracle at the wedding in Cana. Do you remember Jesus' first response to His mother? "When the wine was gone, Jesus' mother said to him, 'They have no more wine.' 'Woman, why do you involve me?' Jesus replied. 'My hour has not yet come'" (John 2:3–4 NIV).

Now let's look at the verbiage He uses with the Samaritan woman at the well.

> "Woman," Jesus replied, "believe me, the hour is coming when you will worship the Father neither on this mountain nor in Jerusalem ... Yet a time is coming and has now come when the true worshipers will worship the Father in the Spirit and in truth, for they are the kind of worshipers the Father seeks." (John 4:21, 23 NIV)

Do you see it? He uses the same line!

Don't miss this: He's saying to the Samaritan woman, "Believe me. The hour is coming when My spirit will be poured out and you'll marry Me." He's telling her that He's met His bride. When Mary had asked Him at the wedding to help fix the wine situation, He was agitated because He couldn't yet marry His bride and share a cup with her.

But now He's telling the Samaritan woman that the hour is coming when He can be betrothed to His bride, and the hour has come when He's met His bride. Again, the Samaritan woman is a representation of the bride of Christ. She symbolizes who Christ came for.

Let's look at other passages that describe who Jesus came for.

> I have not come to call the righteous, but sinners to repentance. (Luke 5:32 NIV)

> On hearing this, Jesus said to them, "It is not the healthy who need a doctor, but the sick. I have not come to call the righteous, but sinners." (Mark 2:17 NIV)

For the Son of Man came to seek and to save the lost. (Luke 19:10 NIV)

The Lord is not slow to fulfill his promise as some count slowness, but is patient toward you, not wishing that any should perish, but that all should reach repentance. (2 Peter 3:9 ESV)

The Spirit of the Lord GOD is upon me, because the LORD has anointed me to bring good news to the poor; he has sent me to bind up the brokenhearted, to proclaim liberty to the captives, and the opening of the prison to those who are bound. (Isaiah 61:1 ESV)

Jesus wants to share a cup with the Samaritan woman and tell her, "You are my bride." Through this encounter, we see that His bride is anyone who is a sinner and needs a Savior. His bride is anyone who has messed it up on their own and needs freedom from the bondage of sin and shame. His bride is anyone who needs Jesus, which is all of us.

Jesus reminds us here that He is our Bridegroom and that if we drink the cup of acceptance and choose to say yes to Him, we'll be washed clean by His blood and set free from the power of darkness. We'll have a seat at His banquet table and a room in His Father's house. We'll be married to Jesus for eternity.

The hour is now, and our time is short. Jesus is offering you His hand in marriage. And believe me, woman, the hour has come for you to accept His offer!

Day 5: I Am He

"I am he." I don't know about you, but this line from Jesus to the Samaritan woman gives me chills. Let's see how this story concludes and what parallels we can draw from it to our spiritual lives today.

Read John 4:21–26.

- Why do you think the woman didn't know she was talking with Jesus?

In these verses, Jesus gives the Samaritan woman a glimpse of His coming Spirit and how that will greatly influence the way all believers will worship. He tells her that an hour is coming when she and her people will worship the Father neither on this mountain nor in Jerusalem. He goes on to say that a time is coming and has now come when the true worshipers will worship the Father in spirit and in truth. Those are the people the Father seeks.

To grasp the full picture of this point, it's important to pause and note that at this time in history, the Samaritans had built a temple of worship to rival the one in Jerusalem. They had a long history of political and religious rivalry. Unfortunately we still see that same attitude of rivalry and division among denominations and churches today. It's easy to get caught up in the wrong issues and become divided.

Jesus is saying here that true worshipers don't focus on where or how they worship in the physical realm, but they worship unified in spirit and in truth. He's saying that we shouldn't focus too much on our different backgrounds, church affiliations, and worship styles, but on the one Lord who unites us.

Jesus wants His church to be whole, not fractured. Why? Because He knows that our spiritual enemy wants the church to be focused solely on division and competition. Besides Jesus Himself, Satan's worst nightmare is a unified bride.

There is one spirit of God, and because He dwells inside us, we're all connected. We can worship together, unify in spirit, and bring God glory. Notice that we're always called "the bride of Christ" (singular), not "the brides of Christ" (plural). Jesus is monogamous, and He's coming for His one bride.

As Christ's church, the way we worship doesn't matter so much as why we worship. Above all else, Jesus desires a pure heart that seeks Him. Remember, we learned before that it's the inside of the cup that needs to be clean.

All across Scripture, we see this common theme that God views things differently than we do. Let's read the following verses and learn more: 1 Samuel 16:7, Psalm 51:10, Matthew 5:8, Hebrews 4:12, Proverbs 21:2, Matthew 15:18–20, and James 4:8.

Knowing this, let's go back to the story of the Samaritan woman. What does Jesus say to her in John 4:26 (NIV)?

Jesus saw her, knew her, loved her, and offered her living water. He proposed to her, and her life was forever changed. I absolutely love the language He uses here. "I, the one speaking to you—I am he." He revealed Himself to her, just as He longs to reveal Himself to you. He's the Bridegroom, and you, my dear, are His bride.

In verses 28–29, we see the woman's response after she learned whom she was speaking to. Her physical needs lost all importance at the knowledge of meeting Christ, so she left her water jar. For the first time in a long time, she felt loved. She found her true love in Jesus!

She was a broken woman who was lost and longing for a love she couldn't seem to find. But after she met her true Bridegroom, she had a purpose and wanted this news to reach her community. She could hardly wait to share what she had learned. She ran to tell others about her experience.

Jesus offered her the true source of life, met her in her desperation, and gave her life new meaning and dignity. He used her to tell others about Him, and He does this for us too. We're never too bad or too broken to be restored and used by Him. When we place our faith in Him, He uses our failures for His good purposes. That's not the end of this story though. It gets even better from here!

Read John 4:39–42.

- What impact did the Samaritan woman's testimony have on her community?

Jesus used this woman to reach many more Samaritans. He came for us sinners in need of a Savior. And when we say yes to Him, He doesn't just change our own lives. He uses us to reach and impact people all around us.

As we wrap up this week, I want you to know that there's an everlasting love that will satisfy your every longing, and it can only be found in Christ. Open your eyes to the Bridegroom before you today. Jesus is revealing Himself to you as the ultimate answer. He's telling you, "I am he."

Group Guide

- Welcome the Group

- Open in Prayer

- Watch Week 5 video found at LaynieTravis.com/willyoumarryme (24:58)

- Go over discussion questions or as many as time allows for:

  1. Read John 4:1–6. Which well did Jesus sit by to take a break from his long journey?
  2. Read Exodus 2:15–21. Where did Moses meet his bride?
  3. What do you think sharing a cup with the Samaritan woman at a popular betrothal scene symbolizes?
  4. What did Jesus say He would give the Samaritan women if she would ask?
  5. Was the Samaritan woman a Jew or a Gentile? Why is this significant?
  6. What does Jesus say is the difference between the well water and His living water? What is the Samaritan woman's response?
  7. What was the Samaritan woman's relationship status?
  8. Compare the language used in John 2:3–4 and John 4:21–23. What similarities do you see? What do you think this means?
  9. Who does the Samaritan woman represent as a whole?
  10. What impact did the Samaritan woman's testimony have on her community?

- Close in Prayer

Going to the Chapel

Day 1: The Rapture

We've learned so far that Jesus is our Bridegroom, we are His bride, and a wedding is coming. Scholars may differ on certain interpretations and timelines regarding this coming wedding and feast, but we can all agree that it's going to happen. Why? Because of the prophecies in the Bible.

A prophecy is the foretelling or prediction of what is to come. The Bible is filled with prophecies because God wants to assure His people about the amazing future that awaits us. He gives us a divine heads-up and puts a vision in our hearts and minds to encourage us and prepare us for future events on His kingdom calendar. He tells us in the Bible of future bliss and future judgment. He wants us to choose Him and avoid the dangers coming to those who reject Him. God gives us free choice but warns us of the consequences of our choices.

Dr. John Walvoord has dedicated more than sixty years of his life studying biblical prophecy and has identified more than a thousand prophecies in the Bible, five hundred of which have already been fulfilled. God tells us how history will wrap up. He gives us the information long before it happens, and we can rest assured that in His perfect timing, it will all come true.

So what does the Bible tell us about this grand future event? Let's look closely today at the future wedding.

> Fear not, little flock, for it is your Father's good pleasure to give you the kingdom. (Luke 12:32 ESV)

> Let not your hearts be troubled. Believe in God; believe also in me. In my Father's house are many rooms. If it were not so, would I have told you that I go to prepare a place for you? And if I go and prepare a place for you, I will come again and will take you to myself, that where I am you may be also. (John 14:1–3 ESV)

> Behold, He is coming with the clouds, and every eye will see Him, even those who pierced Him; and all the tribes of the earth will mourn over Him. So it is to be. Amen. "I am the Alpha and the Omega," says the Lord God, "who is and who was and who is to come, the Almighty." (Revelation 1:7–8 NASB)

Read Revelation 21:1–6.

- What will no longer exist in the new heaven and new earth?

The return of Jesus Christ is prophesied a whopping 329 times in the Bible. The majority of the Bible's prophecies that are yet to be fulfilled concern His second coming. There are 129 prophecies regarding Jesus's first coming, so His return is prophesied almost three times more than His first coming. These numbers can assure us that He is coming again!

Here's one example:

> "Men of Galilee," they said, "why do you stand here looking into the sky? This same Jesus, who has been taken from you into heaven, will come back in the same way you have seen him go into heaven." (Acts 1:11 NIV)

Jesus will come again. According to Tim LaHaye, a popular author on end-time events, the second coming of Christ will occur in two phases, beginning with the rapture of the church. Then at least seven years later, Jesus will physically come to the earth in what LaHaye calls the "Glorious Appearing."

Scholars have many theories regarding the timing of these events, but the truth is that no one knows for sure what it will look like. For this study's sake, I'm going to align with the interpretation in Tim's book *The Merciful God of Prophecy: His Loving Plan for You in the End Times* to help us develop a foundational understanding of these prophecies.

Today we're going to focus primarily on the rapture. This is the first phase of Jesus's return, when Christ will come back for His bride, the universal church. He'll come at a time no one suspects—when God the Father gives the order—and He'll come to snatch His bride out of the earth.

Remember the first week when we studied the Jewish wedding process? When did the bridegroom go and get his bride? He would wait until the bridal chamber was ready and his father would give him the go-ahead. Then and only then would he go and get his bride.

Do you remember what it was called when he went to alert his bride of his coming? Exactly. The procession. He would show up at her house (usually at midnight), blow a *shofar* trumpet, and call out in a loud voice, "Come and meet your bridegroom!"

This gives us a visual picture of what it will look like when Christ, our Bridegroom, comes back for us, His betrothed. Let's take a look.

> For the Lord Himself will descend from heaven with a shout, with the voice of the archangel and with the trumpet of God, and the dead in Christ will rise first. Then we who are alive and remain will be caught up together with them in the clouds to meet the Lord in the air, and so we shall always be with the Lord. Therefore, comfort one another with these words. (1 Thessalonians 4:16–18 NASB)

God the Father will tell Jesus, "Go and get your bride." Then the Lord Himself, our Bridegroom, will descend from heaven. With a shout and the call of a trumpet, we'll meet Him in the sky. It'll be at an hour that we don't expect. And just as the Jewish bride wanted to be found ready, we too need to be ready to meet our Bridegroom face-to-face.

In the rapture, the spirits of already deceased believers will receive glorified bodies. Those of us who are alive on earth will also receive glorified bodies and go to meet our bridegroom in the air. I firmly believe that we'll be raptured up to heaven with Jesus before the great tribulation occurs. The tribulation will be a time of unprecedented evil on earth when the Antichrist will rule for seven years. This is another prophecy that is yet to be fulfilled.

The church, also known as the bride of Christ, will be taken up out of the world during this time of judgment. Those of us who have accepted Jesus's invitation to be betrothed to Him will go with Him to heaven to attend the great wedding, while those remaining on earth will endure a dark and brutal time of judgment.

We can look back throughout the Bible and see that God consistently rescued His people from destruction. For example, he saved Noah and his family from the flood. He saved Lot from the destruction of Sodom and Gomorrah, and He saved Rahab and her family from the destruction of Jericho. This leads me to believe that He'll save us, His believers, from the coming horrors of the tribulation too. "Jesus, who rescues us from the wrath to come" (1 Thessalonians 1:10 NASB).

I know it sounds cruel that those who aren't betrothed to Christ will remain on earth during this horrific time, but love always offers free choice. Love without free choice isn't really love. Just as the Jewish bride had the choice of whether or not to accept her bridegroom, Jesus gives us all a choice. He chooses each of us, and He offers us each a personal invitation to become His bride.

If we say yes, we become personally betrothed to Him. We become a member of the universal bride made up of all believers, just as a university has one student body consisting of many individual students. Jesus knocks on the door of each of our hearts and asks to come in and dine with us. He wants us for His own and loves each of us as if there were only one of us.

Let's see what else Scripture has to say about the rapture.

> Now, brothers and sisters, about times and dates we do not need to write to you, for you know very well that the day of the Lord will come like a thief in the night. (1 Thessalonians 5:1–2 NIV)

> You also must be ready, because the Son of Man will come at an hour when you do not expect him. (Luke 12:40 NIV)

Like a thief in the night, the rapture will be sudden and unexpected—much like the Jewish bridegroom would come at a time the bride didn't expect. The bride would then hope to find herself ready with her wedding garments hung and spotless.

Do you see the parallels? Jesus is giving us a picture so we can understand and be ready.

After Jesus comes and "snatches" up His bride, He'll take us to His Father's house, where we'll celebrate "the marriage supper of the Lamb." This wedding and feast will be beyond anything we could ever imagine. It'll put the royal wedding to shame.

This celebration with Jesus will be holy, magnificent, beautiful, majestic, and full of love and joy, and it will be fun! He brings joy, life, renewal, beauty, and love. All we have to do is say yes and be ready.

Day 2: The Glorious Appearing

Today we're going to discuss the second phase of the second coming of Christ, which is known as the "Glorious Appearing." After Jesus marries His bride, He'll return to earth to reign with her in the Millennial Kingdom. I know this all sounds like we're in a fairy tale, but it's what's in the Bible, people. He'll come back to earth as a mighty warrior, and all the earth will see Him in all His glory.

Let's read the following passages to see what Scripture says about this appearing: Matthew 24:29–30, Revelation 1:7, and Revelation 19:11–16.

The "Glorious Appearing" will occur at the end of the horrific seven-year tribulation. Jesus will come again with a mission to set up an everlasting kingdom. The world will literally come face-to-face with the One they rejected. Every eye will see Him and mourn Him.

In the second phase of His return, Jesus will set up a kingdom on earth where He'll reign with us, His bride. He'll be the head of this new kingdom, just like a husband is the head of the home.

Jesus came to earth the first time as a lamb that was led to slaughter, but He'll return as a lion—bold and fierce. He's coming again and will reign in the Millennial Kingdom for one thousand years. We'll be with Him, ruling alongside Him.

This may sound strange, but it's the truth of the Bible. God is the creator, and He exists in an eternal realm. He knows the complete story and how it will end. He's the Alpha and the Omega—the beginning and the end. He set time in motion, and we're always moving forward in His timeline until we reach the end. It's imperative for us to understand that the clock is ticking.

Jesus wants us for Himself, and He has magnificent plans for us that we can't even fathom from our limited and worldly perspective. We can give ourselves permission to dream, hope, and look forward to a romantic fairy-tale bliss. It's real and otherworldly, and in a world full of disappointment, we can know that in the end, we won't be disappointed.

Every good dream will come true, every need will be met, and every heartache will be mended. What's coming is better than we could even imagine! The rapture, the wedding, the Glorious Appearing, and the new heaven and the new earth will all result in a place of perfect unity and peace with Jesus, our husband and king. He'll reign on the throne in a world with no pain.

Read Revelation 21:1–8.

- How does the promise of this new heaven and earth make you feel?

- Is this scene easy or difficult for you to imagine? Why?

Jesus is coming, and He wants to come take us with Him to marry us. He'll protect His bride from the tribulation that will last for seven years. We'll be in heaven with our Bridegroom celebrating our marriage until we return with Him to earth. He's spelling this all out for us in His Word.

He wants you there. Trust me. You'll want to be there too.

Day 3: Two Become One

Today I want to reiterate the importance of the marriage model that God designed from the beginning. Marriage gives us a physical picture that we can grasp onto to help us understand the intimate dynamics of the love relationship Jesus wants to have with us.

Read Genesis 2:4–25.

- Why did God create a helper for Adam?

- How did Adam and Eve feel about their nakedness?

God designed marriage. He formed Adam from the dust of the earth and then formed Eve from his rib. Genesis 2:24 (BSB) tells us, "For this reason, a man will leave his father and mother and be united to his wife, and they shall become one flesh." What does this tell us? Adam and Eve were created to be married, united, and in full submission to one another. That was God's design from the beginning.

They were married, they became one flesh, and they were naked and unashamed. Have you ever seen the reality show called *Naked and Afraid*? I haven't either. (And I don't ever want to.) But the title definitely makes me laugh. It also sums up how we often feel about intimacy with each other and at times with God. We're afraid to be exposed. We feel unsafe, and it's hard in that state to be vulnerable.

Adam and Eve started out completely exposed to God and to each other, but they felt safe. Wouldn't this be amazing? Not the naked in public part (ha!), but the feeling that you're perfectly and completely loved. You don't have to try to hide who you are. You're free from all fear and shame. Before sin entered the world, Adam and Eve didn't know or understand shame. Satan deceived them, and as sin entered the world, so did shame.

Read Genesis 3:1–11.

- How did the serpent first deceive Eve?

- What happened to Adam and Eve when their eyes were opened?

- What is God's response to them?

Jesus came to earth to save us from our sin and take away our shame. Satan, our accuser, exposes us and embarrasses us. He wants us to hide from God and feel ashamed. He wants us to feel isolated and alone in our guilt. Jesus fights for us and purifies us to cover our shame. He wants us to be completely vulnerable and open with Him and feel safe. He desires to be joined as one with us for eternity.

I believe this physical picture of marriage mirrors our spiritual relationship with Christ. When we get married in this life, we're bound together with our husbands and become one flesh, both physically and emotionally. We become fully submitted to one another. Physically, we're joined together in the most intimate act of sex, and emotionally, we're joined as we lean on one another and battle through the ups and downs of life together.

As the bride of Jesus, our spiritual intimacy with Him won't be a sexual union, but like the act of sex, we'll reach full spiritual intimacy with Christ. We'll be completely "naked" before Him and feel no shame. Our union in the physical mirrors our union with Christ in the spiritual.

God's design of marriage is a picture of perfect intimacy and pleasure between a husband and wife. Our spiritual union with Christ will be an exotic pleasure in Him that we simply can't comprehend in this physical realm. It will exceed any earthly pleasure we've ever known.

Jesus sees us and knows us as we've never been known before because in Him, we're completely accepted and loved. Our marriages here on earth are stained with sin, and as a result of living in a fallen world, we experience pain and heartache, even in the happiest of unions.

In our spiritual glorified bodies, there will be no sin or shame that stains our marriage relationship with Jesus. We'll be presented to Him as a pure bride, washed completely clean of sin. When we become spiritually betrothed to Christ here on earth, meaning that we have the indwelling of His spirit, we're set apart as His bride and await the eternal bliss of being married to Him forever. It'll be better than any love we've ever known.

God designed earthly marriage, and He blesses marriage. It was no coincidence that the first miracle Jesus performed on earth was at a wedding! Just as we learned with that first miracle, He saves the best for last. In your relationship with Christ, the best is yet to come.

To sum it all up, in the beginning, we see the first example of a marriage relationship in Adam and Eve. The two become one flesh, and they were naked and unashamed. When sin entered the world, they felt ashamed and exposed.

God clothed Adam and Eve with flesh, and Jesus clothes us with robes of righteousness. These are our wedding garments, and they're fit for a bride. He brings us into the shade of His tent where we're safe and protected. Just as Adam and Eve became one, we become one with Christ when we accept His invitation to drink of the living water. His spirit comes to take up residence within our souls, connecting us to Him for all eternity.

We await the hour when we'll meet our bridegroom face-to-face as husband and wife. What a moment that will be!

Day 4: It Is Finished, My Bride!

When Jesus breathed His last breath on the cross, He uttered the words, "It is finished." I love the way this verse reads in The Passion Translation, "When he had sipped the sour wine, he said, 'It is finished, my bride!' Then he bowed his head and surrendered his spirit to God" (John 19:30 TPT).

The Hebrew word for "finished" used in this verse is the word *kalah*, a homonym that can mean "finished" or "bride." I think this interpretation accurately depicts who Jesus accomplished this great and gruesome sacrifice for. He endured the brutal suffering thinking about His bride—you.

While the nails were being hammered into His hands and the crown of thorn pushed into His scalp, He had you on His mind. He did this so each of us can be free from sin and death and one day be married to Him.

When it was over and He gave up His spirit, Jesus spoke the words, "It is finished, my bride!" He was essentially saying, "I did this for you so I could have you, and now I can!" The power of these words and this monumental moment will never fully be understood. This is what true love looks like. He bore it all for us so He could have us as His bride.

Take a moment right now to prayerfully reflect on these verses:

> Let us fix our eyes on Jesus, the author and perfecter of our faith, who for the joy set before Him endured the cross, scorning its shame, and sat down at the right hand of the throne of God. (Hebrews 12:2 BSB)

> This is how we know what love is: Jesus Christ laid down his life for us. And we ought to lay down our lives for our brothers and sisters. (1 John 3:16 NIV)

> Husbands, love your wives, just as Christ loved the church and gave himself up for her. (Ephesians 5:25 NIV)

For the joy set before Him, Jesus endured the suffering of the cross. He knew what was waiting on the other side of the cross: you and me. You're worth it to Him. Every beating from the whip, every blow to the face, and every word of shame and ridicule, He took it all for you.

I love how The Passion Translation commentary explains Jesus's continued work in our lives.

> Although the completed work of salvation was finished on the cross, he continues to work through his church today to extend God's kingdom realm on the earth and glorify the Father through us. He continues to work in us to accomplish all that his cross and resurrection have purchased for us, his bride. (John 19:30 TPT footnote)

We, the church, are the bride of Christ. He refers to "His bride" in a feminine context, but both male and female believers alike are "married" to Christ when we surrender our lives to Him. Our marriage to Christ is not a gender issue, but a full submission and eternal relationship issue.

As we've learned this week, our marriage to Christ is like an earthly marriage in that Christ is the head, just as a husband is the spiritual head of his wife. In heaven, we'll be fully submitted to Him in our glorified bodies. We'll see Him and know Him face-to-face, and our relationship with Him will reach complete unity.

Let's wrap up by reading and focusing on these two passages: Hosea 2:19 and 1 Corinthians 15:50–57.

Jesus laid down His life for us and gave Himself up for us. It is finished. His love mission has been accomplished—and even with His last breath, He called out to His bride, pleading with us to say yes to Him for eternity.

Why? Because He loves you.

Day 5: Newlyweds

I can't believe it, girls! We're on the last day! We made it! I sincerely hope you've developed a new and deeper understanding of the bride-and-bridegroom relationship depicted all throughout the Bible.

I want to end our study with a look at what it'll be like to be married to Christ. We only have a limited view and picture of what's to come, so we can't fully understand it all in our human minds, but what the Bible does reveal whets our appetites for a world we can't even begin to imagine. It'll be indescribable and unbelievable.

Let's read this verse to get a sneak peek:

> And Jesus said to them, "The sons of this age marry and are given in marriage, but those who are considered worthy to attain to that age and to the resurrection from the dead neither marry nor are given in marriage, for they cannot die anymore, because they are equal to angels and are sons of God, being sons of the resurrection." (Luke 20:34–36 ESV)

What Jesus means here is that we won't be married in heaven as we are on this earth. Marriage to another person passes away in the age to come. We're immortal like angels and will be married to Christ. He's the one and only groom. He's our king, and we'll be joined to Him in the supernatural. It'll look different than marriage here on earth, and it'll exceed all our greatest expectations.

Let's dive in more: Genesis 1:26–30, Romans 6:5–7, 2 Timothy 2:11–13, and Ephesians 2:1–10.

God created us male and female in His own image. In the garden of Eden, God made mankind ruler over the land and the beasts of the field. As sin entered the world though, we lost our ability to fully rule the earth.

God, in His love and mercy, saved us from our sins through grace and raises us up with Him. He frees us from our bondage to sin and seats us in the heavenly places with Christ. On the cross, He showed us the surpassing riches of His grace—a true gift from God. All we have to do is say yes to receiving His spirit and we can become alive in Christ.

When we get married to Jesus, we'll go with Him as He comes back to the earth in the "Glorious Appearing" after the great tribulation. We'll come back with Him in all our splendor as His bride, and we'll be given full authority to reign with Him in the new heaven and the new earth.

Read Revelation 19:7–14.

- What are the bride and armies of heaven both wearing?

- What does it represent? What is Jesus wearing?

- What does it represent?

As we just read, we'll be right there with Jesus. We'll be dressed in bright and clean white linen, and we'll be ready to reign with Him. We'll have power and positions of great authority. We'll be like kings and queens ruling the new earth.

Read 1 Corinthians 6:2–3.

- Who will the Lord's people judge?

As the bride of Christ, we'll sit on thrones alongside our Savior and Bridegroom and enjoy all that is His. We'll rule and reign with Him in all power and love during the Millennial Kingdom.

Last but not least, we'll be beautiful. Girls, let's not pretend that this doesn't matter to us! We all long to be beautiful. Just look at this world we live in: Being young and beautiful has taken on its own form of idolatry. We're addicted to it. Sadly, in our culture, outward beauty often takes precedence over inward beauty.

It's important for us to always keep in mind that God made us in His image. Whether we think it or not, we're lovely and gorgeous to Him. The standard of beauty here on earth is perverted, but God designed us and has uniquely gifted each of us. He knows us intimately. Scripture tells us that even the hairs on our heads are numbered. He loves us. He sees us. He desires us.

Living in this fallen world where we do get older and our bodies grow feebler, we can be confident that the spirit of God in us is growing stronger and more beautiful day by day.

We'll reach our full peak of beauty in His kingdom, and we'll be gorgeous! Words fail to describe what we'll look like.

We won't be a humble, feeble bride. We'll be a mighty, strong, and breathtakingly beautiful glorified body—pure as snow. We'll shine in the love of our Savior and be glorious in His presence.

Let's revisit that girl we saw at the beginning of this study, the one at the wedding.

She's magnificent. She's running free. She's finally arrived and can't contain her joy and passion. She's not shrinking back, but sprinting down the aisle in all her splendor and beauty. She's fierce and powerful, relentless in her pursuit to get to Him, Jesus.

He's waiting and watching in awe. He's bursting with pride at the sight of her. His love penetrates the air. He's a warrior who has fought for her and won. She sees Him facing her and knows that it was all worth the wait. This moment erases all her past pain, heartache, loss, and disappointment.

All that she's ever questioned in life suddenly makes sense. She understands the why of every question she's ever asked and every no she's ever received. She understands His purpose for her and realizes that she's finally home. She's safe. She's loved. She's wanted.

That she is you! Our day and hour to be betrothed to Christ is here. He's asking you. No, He's begging you to be His own. He's after you with a relentless pursuit. Say yes, and you'll find Him welcoming you with open arms.

You'll be the girl running to Him and living in a beautiful, endless dream. All pain and loss will be gone, and there will only be a faint memory of the world we used to know. It won't haunt or hold you anymore. In Him, you are fully free.

Jesus, our Bridegroom, is calling for you. He's down on one knee, asking you to share the cup of acceptance and be betrothed and promised to Him forever.

Say yes! The best is yet to come!

Group Guide

- Welcome the Group

- Open in Prayer

- Watch Week 6 video found at LaynieTravis.com/willyoumarryme (28:27)

- Go over discussion questions or as many as time allows for:

  1. What is a prophecy?
  2. How many prophecies of Christ's second coming are mentioned in the Bible?
  3. Read 1 Thessalonians 4:16–17. According to Tim LaHaye, what are the two phases of the second coming of Christ?
  4. Read 1 Thessalonians 5:1–2 and Luke 12:40. How do these prophecies compare to the Jewish wedding process?
  5. Read Matthew 24:29–30, Revelation 1:7, and Revelation 19:11–16. What happens after the rapture and after Jesus marries His bride?
  6. Read Revelation 21:1–8. How does the promise of this new heaven and earth make you feel? Is this scene easy or difficult for you to imagine? Why?
  7. How does marriage as we know it on earth mirror our spiritual marriage to Christ both now and in eternity?
  8. Read Ephesians 5:35 and Hebrews 12:2. What joy was set before Jesus that compelled Him to complete His mission for us?
  9. Read John 19:30 TPT. How does reading Jesus's final words on the cross—"It is finished, my bride!"—take on a new meaning for you after reading this study?
  10. In your own words, what does it mean to be betrothed to Christ in this life? What does it mean to be married to Christ for all eternity?

- Close in Prayer

Printed in the United States
By Bookmasters